To Linn —
God Bless!!!
You Abundantly!!!

STEFAN RYBAK

THE
SHADOW
ON MY
HEART

FAITH. FAMILY. FORGIVENESS.

08·20·21

The Shadow On My Heart
Faith. Family. Forgiveness.

Author: Stefan Rybak
Editor: Marla McKenna
Associate Editor: Griffin Mill
Proofreader: Lyda Rose Haerle
Cover Design and Interior Layout: Michael Nicloy

All images contained in this book are owned by the author.

ISBN-13: 978-1945907-73-9

Published by Nico 11 Publishing & Design,
Mukwonago, Wisconsin
www.nico11publishing.com

Be well read.

Quantity and wholesale order requests can be emailed to:
mike@nico11publishing.com
or can be made by phone: 217.779.9677

Printed in The United States of America

Author's Note #1:

Special thanks to Yusuf Toropov for his invaluable assistance with the writing of this book. He worked with me patiently and diligently, and helped me bring all of the pieces of this story together in a kind, loving, most caring, and professional way. If you've ever dreamed of writing a book but didn't know how to get started, I highly recommend that you reach out to Yusuf. His email address is: iwordsmithsupport@gmail.com.

Author's Note #2:

I also wish to thank my publisher, Michael Nicloy, and editor, Marla McKenna, for all of their work on this project. I deeply appreciate the enthusiasm they showed after reading the original manuscript, and all of the faith and encouragement they've generously provided throughout the process of making this book a reality.

Author's Note #3:

A portion of the proceeds of the sale of this book will be donated to Jane's Home for senior-age, developmentally-disabled adults, an IRS-registered 501(c)(3) non-profit organization. Support services include, but are not limited to, private housing in the community, 24-hour supervised care, and assistance with daily living. For more information, please see the website www.JanesHome.org.

- Stefan

I dedicate this book to the four most important people in my life: my wonderful wife Victoria, and our three beautiful and dynamic adult children, Nicole, Alexandra, and Stefan Michael.

My heart beats for them.

FOREWORD
BY MARTIN PAGE

What a beautiful, tender, spiritual book this is. Naked, honest, spiritually-charged. It's a letter to a friend, a personal diary of redemption, a lamentation on recovery and the tough journey it takes to get there. Not only recovery of the physical body, but recovery of the soul.

This is also a memoir of prayer and the power to reach beyond oneself. It's a narrative about healing, and about how we all can succumb to the dark side but still have the chance of inner spiritual recovery.

I think many, many people will benefit from reading this book. They will connect with and be touched by a powerful story that's written with eloquence and insight. Stefan's words will, no doubt, help inspire and empower many people on their own untidy journey through life.

Martin Page is a world-renowned, award-winning hit songwriter, whose songwriting credits include the #1 hits "We Built This City" (for Starship), "These Dreams" (for Heart), and "In the House of Stone and Light" (for Martin Page).

THE SHADOW
ON MY HEART

CHAPTER ONE

The first and most important thing that you need to understand is that there was an unspoken, non-negotiable rule that I always had to follow when I was growing up. It was more important than my wife not having the time to call 911 for an ambulance for me. More important than whether I made it to the emergency room in time. And, even more important than what the Nazis did to my mother. That rule was short and sweet. My mother made sure you caught hell if you ever came close to ignoring it.

The rule was: Family First. Always.

It sounds simple, and I guess technically it is, but it's easier to break that rule than you might imagine.

About that trip to the emergency room—I was not an absentee dad or an absentee husband. I coached my son's baseball and basketball teams. I was in the audience for my daughter's recitals and school plays. I didn't leave people who counted on me wondering where I was or what I was doing. I didn't go out carousing. I'm a family-focused person, and I'm pretty sure my wife Victoria would back me up on that. But I was working a lot.

I had to.

To a certain extent, managing radio stations can be fun and glamorous, but pushing myself through a seemingly endless series of high-stress, 60-plus-hour workweeks to do it was like running in a non-stop marathon. I had little time to catch my breath. Then, in 2012, at the age of 54, I made a "leap of faith" career move. I decided I was going to start my own media consulting company and a couple of other businesses that appealed to the entrepreneur in me. It was a chance to work for myself and make my own rules, which felt great. But I was also responsible for bringing in every penny of income. Gulp. Suddenly, those 60-hour workweeks turned into 70- to 80-hour workweeks more often than I wanted to admit.

Yes, the bet paid off. In financial terms, I guess you could say that I was successful. I suppose you could also say because of the success, I provided a very nice lifestyle for my family. I assumed the price tag for that lifestyle was well worth it. I thought by choosing a hectic, fast-paced, professional lifestyle that I was putting my family first.

* * *

My wife Victoria, my daughters Nicole and Alexandra, and my son and namesake Stefan were the reasons I worked such long hours. That's how I justified it to myself, anyway, and how I explained it to my mother, even though she was no longer with me.

Family first, Stefan. Always. And remember, God is your friend, and His plan is the best plan.

I know, Mama. I know.

I'm not so sure I did know, though.

The possibility that I was taking my family life for granted and that my entire world was about to turn upside down didn't enter my mind that holiday season of December 2015, when I was a month away from my 58th birthday. I didn't stop to ask myself whether I paid too much attention to work, and maybe not enough attention to the everyday blessings that are worth far more than hitting revenue goals. I was too busy to think about things like that. I was complacent. I thought I was following my mother's rule to the letter. But there were a whole lot of things I didn't know in December 2015. I didn't know that I should have been more grateful for my family and my life, and that I should have spent more time with my wife and kids. I didn't know the importance of slowing down to take a deep breath and relax. I didn't know how deep my mother's love went. And I didn't realize that I was about to get hammered hard by fate.

* * *

If you ever have an unexpected turn of events in your life, if you ever happen to feel shattered, if you ever wonder whether there's any point in not giving up, then I hope that you have someone like my mother around to help you. If this book helps you, then it'll have been worth writing. And whatever corner of heaven my mother might be in right now, I hope that she reads these words and smiles.

I've got it now, Mama. "Family first." I promise.

I built a career in the media and entertainment industry, which is a pretty exciting place. I've done a lot of things other people tell me they wish they could have done. People often ask me what it's like meeting pop stars, speaking on the radio, appearing on television, writing a column in the newspaper, and rising to the heights of a successful media executive—all of which I've done at one point or another. Here's my answer: It's not unlike the line from that old Eagles song about rushing down the highway and not caring whether or not you get lost.

You can all too easily become hooked on that way of life. There are so many exhilarating moments and fringe benefits that you start to imagine that they're what normal is supposed to be—discovering songs that ended up being bit smash hits on the music charts? Sure! Getting tickets to more shows and concerts than most people can imagine? Why not! Enjoying backstage passes for meet-and-greets with A-list performers? That's an everyday part of the job!

You can get used to that kind of thing. It's a heady lifestyle but it comes at a high price. You may end up driving yourself through the day in a rush. When you get home, you're not entirely present. You're decompressing, but just for a moment. In your head, you're gearing up for the next highway, getting ready to hit the next on-ramp.

In a way, living that kind of life is even worse than a real drug addiction because it can last a lot longer. You can keep this habit up for years before you realize the toll it's taken on you.

There's a little table right next to the desk in my home office. On that table are my mother's rosary beads, the glasses she was wearing when she died in 2013, a photograph of her when she was a young woman, and her Bible. The Bible has many underlined verses. Among those verses are the Polish words for "Thy will be done." The last Christmas card I received from my mother before she died is also on this table.

On the evening of December 19, 2015, I was sitting alone in my home office. It was a Saturday; I'd worked all day and missed dinner with my family. I was eating alone and thinking about that Christmas card. I had found it that morning while I was rummaging around in a box looking for something else.

The inscription read: *Dear Stefan and Great Family – Love You All! Mama Babcia.* Babcia is the Polish word for grandmother.

What a nice coincidence, I thought. *Finding that card just six days before Christmas. It's almost like she's trying to talk to me.*

I turned on the computer to check my work email one more time before spending some evening time with my family. I had some projects in play, and I was still hoping to make my year-end sales numbers, which were, as always, aggressive. Checking my email would only take a few minutes.

Family first, Stefan. Always.

I know, Mama. I know.

* * *

When I looked up from my computer, an hour and a half had passed, and everyone else in the house was getting ready for bed.

I missed "family time." Again.

* * *

Sunday, December 20, 2015, 8 am

I'm lying in bed. My wife is still sleeping. I'm reading the Bible while waiting for Victoria to wake up so we can go downstairs and have breakfast together. Inspired by that card from my mother, I'm reading the Gospel of Luke, Chapter 1, Verse 38, the words of the Blessed Virgin Mary;

Behold, I am the handmaid of the Lord. May it be done to me according to your word. It was one of my mother's favorite verses.

Suddenly, out of nowhere, it's like someone has pushed a button at the very core of me. There's incredible pressure in the center of my chest. I feel like I'm plunging down the world's biggest roller coaster ride, and a balloon is blowing up inside of me.

My wife hears me moan loudly. I pass out for a few seconds. When I come to, I'm sweating profusely, as if I'd just gotten done running a marathon. My heart is beating erratically, at what feels like about a thousand miles an hour. It feels like it's going to burst right out of my chest.

My first instinct is to jump out of bed. But my legs are like rubber, and I collapse to the floor.

I yell to my wife, "Something's seriously wrong! Take me to the emergency room right away!"

Victoria jumps out of bed, grabs her phone and starts to dial 911.

I shout, "No! We don't have time to wait for the ambulance. The hospital is three-minutes away. We need to drive there right now!" Don't ask me how I knew the ambulance would take too long. I just did.

How I got downstairs and into the car is a complete blur to me now. All I can remember is Victoria behind the wheel, flooring the accelerator.

We raced to the emergency room.

CHAPTER
TWO

The E.R. was a whirlwind of hectic activity and constant noise. My heart was beating wildly. I tried hard to focus on calming myself down.

When the doctor announced that what I experienced at the house was not a heart attack, I felt relieved, somewhat. "It was a cardiac episode," he said, "of an unknown cause."

What the heck is a cardiac episode? That's the question we wanted answered. After six hours of testing and monitoring, the best response we could get from the emergency room medical staff was this: "It obviously has something to do with your heart, Mr. Rybak. While we know for certain that it wasn't a heart attack, we can't tell you at this exact moment exactly what's going on. It could be several different things. For right now, the goal is to stabilize your heartbeat, but you need to see a cardiologist first thing tomorrow morning so he can begin the process of figuring this out."

With my overall condition stabilized, they sent me home with explicit instructions to rest, not go anywhere, and take it easy.

Take it easy? How was I supposed to do that? In all my life, I'd never fainted before, never had my heart beating so wildly, never collapsed to the floor because my legs felt like jello. I had no idea what was going on. That was not a comfortable place for me. Whatever was happening, I knew my body was giving me signs that weren't good.

Over the next five weeks or so, I consulted with multiple doctors and took what seemed like every heart test known to medical science. They all told me the same thing: something serious had happened, but they weren't sure what it was.

Another fainting episode occurred on January 21, 2016, my 58th birthday, causing tension, anxiousness, and confusion to win out over what should have been a happy, upbeat celebration. Through all of this, I felt lousy. I had no energy; I felt constantly lightheaded and drained. My heartbeat was erratic. It was a scary time, with more questions unanswered.

All the uncertainty shook me to the core. How could I make a living and continue to support and provide for my family with my health heading in the wrong direction?

Good news from the doctors would be great. Bad news, well, I'd have to figure out a way to handle that. Somehow.

But *no* news, no clear indication of what the hell was going on inside my body, was torture.

Every new day was supposed to be the day we got some answers. That day refused to come.

At some point (I don't know exactly when), I realized something was pushing me forward through this dark time; it was something I couldn't define. It was a sense of purpose, and it had to do with my mother. Every night, after reading the Bible in bed, as I drifted off to sleep, I found myself thinking of that verse she had loved. I could almost hear her saying, "God's will be done."

And the restless, confusing uncertainty, the desperate quest for answers would recede. Until morning, anyway.

✳ ✳ ✳

Tuesday, January 26, 2016, the day that the answers finally came, was one of the toughest days of my life.

Victoria and I were sitting in Dr. Leonard Girardi's office. He was the Chief Heart Surgeon at Weill Cornell Heart Institute in New York City—one of the leading heart centers in the world. Dr. Girardi walked in, hung up two x-rays, flicked on the light, and said, "Mr. Rybak, you're very seriously ill. You have bicuspid aortic valve disease, a large aortic aneurysm, and need open heart surgery as soon as possible, within the next week or so. No more than two weeks. It *has* to be done soon. There's no running away from this."

I felt a rush of warmth in my face, an instant sweat on my body, and suddenly a very dry mouth. I gulped hard, and said, "What?"

Dr. Girardi went on, "You have a genetic deformity of the aortic valve, the main artery that distributes blood to your body. You've had this since the moment you were born, but the symptoms didn't emerge until now. Less than two-percent of the entire human population has this disorder. As fate would have it, you're part of that two percent."

Completely stunned, I reached out for my wife's hand at the exact moment she reached for mine.

Pointing to an x-ray image, Dr. Girardi said, "The reason you are fainting is that this valve, which has been defective all your life, is failing to the point where it's now cutting off the blood flow to the rest of your body. It is an extremely dangerous condition."

Victoria squeezed my hand tight.

"Heart attack, stroke, incapacitation, and death are real possibilities," he went on to explain. "That valve needs to be replaced as soon as possible."

He pointed to another X-ray. "See this shadow?"

I nodded.

"That's not a shadow. It's an aneurysm on your aorta, the largest blood vessel in the body. The aneurysm is a bulge which weakens the aortic wall. It's a side effect of the bicuspid valve disease. Right now, that thing is 5.1 centimeters in diameter, which is considered medically dangerous. If it bursts, you'll be dead in about 20 or 30 seconds. You won't even have time to call 911."

Victoria and I were still clutching hands when I asked Dr. Girardi, "Are you sure?"

The doctor looked me in the eye.

"Mr. Rybak, here's what I'm sure of. You need to have this surgery done within the next week. Two weeks at most. If you wait any longer, you're taking your life into your hands."

Victoria and I looked at each other in disbelief. I looked back at Dr. Girardi and asked him to tell me about what the surgery would entail.

"The way this operation is done, Mr. Rybak, is we first put you under heavy anesthesia, cut open your chest, then saw your breastbone in half and pull everything open so that we can get to your heart, which is in a protective casing. We then cut that casing open and do what needs to be done. Because your heart can't be beating while we're operating on it, we'll stop it, and during this time, you'll be kept alive by a heart-lung machine."

Cut me open, saw my breastbone in half, and stop my heart while a heart-lung machine keeps me alive. I still couldn't believe what I was hearing, and by the shocked look on Victoria's face, I knew that she was also having a hard time taking it all in.

"So, what do we do now?" I managed to stammer.

Dr. Girardi replied, "See the lady at the front desk who schedules my surgeries. Take the next available opening I have, preferably for next week, and then go home and clear your schedule for at least three months. You're not going to feel like doing too much of anything for at least that length of time. I also suggest that you contact your attorney to make sure that your final paperwork is in order."

"My final paperwork? You mean my will?"

"Yes."

There was a long pause. Then Dr. Girardi said, "Mr. Rybak, I don't know if you are a man of faith, but if you are, I recommend that you speak with your priest or minister or rabbi, or whomever you consider your spiritual mentor or guide, because this an extremely serious procedure you're coming in for. I am not telling you this to frighten you any more than you already are. I'm saying this because I'm going to be operating in God's territory, and whenever I do that, I want my patients as prepared as they can possibly be."

CHAPTER
THREE

It's half-past 10 in the morning on Tuesday, January 26, 2016, and I've just been diagnosed with not one, but two life-threatening heart problems. Before I even left the doctor's office, I found myself thinking about my mother.

I reminded myself that if she could go through all of the things that she'd gone through in her life, and keep "family first," then I needed to find some way to handle my own situation. But, I wasn't sure if I could live up to my mother's example. Deep down, though, I knew I had to try.

I scheduled the surgery for the following week.

Holding Victoria's hand tightly, we left the doctor's office. As we entered the elevator and made our way out to the car, we were both in a daze. There was no way I could drive home, so she took the wheel. I could barely speak, never mind drive through the busy New York City traffic. The moment she let go of my hand, I wished she hadn't.

That ride home took forever. Victoria and I stared at the road ahead in stunned silence. Neither of us could speak—words escaped us.

For the last 5-plus weeks, we'd both known that something was wrong with me physically, but had no idea the seriousness of my illness. When Dr. Girardi gave me his stunning diagnosis and told us how soon he wanted me in for the surgery, we quickly had to come to terms with the magnitude of my problem. In just a few days, I would undergo major heart surgery. It was like someone had flipped an hourglass on us, with the sand quickly sifting through, and neither of us could do anything but watch the sand fall.

As the highway rumbled beneath us, I looked out the passenger window and stared blankly at all the New York landmarks. The 59th Street Bridge, the United Nations Building, and the Midtown Tunnel. Usually, when going in or out of the city, seeing these and other familiar sites would usually lift my spirits, because we loved New York, but they weren't doing anything for me today. I was scared beyond anything I'd ever felt before.

Through the fear, however, I heard my mother's voice, *God is your friend, Stefan. Trust Him. He will take care of you, no matter what. And always be grateful for everything you have.*

What I felt like saying was, "Be grateful, for *this*?" How could I possibly express any gratitude in such a messy situation?

At that moment, we passed the Unisphere from the 1964 World's Fair. Before I realized what was happening, a smile started spreading across my face. Seeing that iconic globe reminded me of a trip my family had taken to that World's Fair when I was young. It was before my father left my mother. I recalled all of us having a great time together and thought about my parents enjoying each other's company that day, laughing and joking around.

Well, I could be grateful for that memory.

Maybe this was Mama talking to me somehow. What else could I be grateful for?

I closed my eyes and pondered that question. At least now I *knew* why I had been experiencing such a complete drain of energy, and why I felt so dizzy and lightheaded. That was something to be grateful for. And at least the prep period would be short. That was another reason to be thankful. I could be grateful I didn't have a lot of time on my hands between diagnosis and surgery. The short timeline gave me less time to panic. And panicking was what I felt like doing at this point. My mortality was staring me straight in the face. What could I possibly do in the face of this enormous adversity *besides* panic?

Keep busy, maybe. That was something else I could be grateful for—the chance to create one of my famous "to-do" lists.

When we got home, I decided to try to busy myself with identifying all the new "to-do" items in my world. I made a list and read it out loud to Victoria.

Talk to my lawyer.

Get my will in order.

Speak to the priest.

Talk to my business associates.

Victoria looked me in the eye and said, "We need to talk to the kids first. That should be at the top of the list."

＊　＊　＊

Alexandra and Stefan still live with us, so we started with them. My wife and I sat them down when we got home. Victoria said, "Daddy has something to say," and looked over at me.

I took a deep breath and began.

"I'm very sick and need a serious heart operation, and—"

My throat choked shut. I began to cry. Hard. I hadn't even made it through the first sentence before the tears had taken over.

Victoria reached out for my hand, and I kept going, my voice rough and heavy, explaining what I could, to the best of my ability. It would be a very invasive heart operation. One of the best heart surgeons in the world would be doing it. He would have to complete not one, but two procedures, a valve replacement, and an aortic aneurysm repair, hoping to fix a coronary disease that I had my whole life but never known about until this day.

"There's really only one shot at getting it right," I said, trying to hold back yet another flood of tears. "There are so many possible complications, but I must go through with it. There's no other choice."

Then my emotional dam burst. My tears turned into loud, uncontrolled sobs. I had been doing my best to show my kids how brave I was, but bravery was my weakest strength at that moment. I couldn't even look at my kids. I could only look at the floor. I've always tried to show my family great strength during challenging times, but at this moment all I could do was cry. My kids had never seen me cry before.

The room fell silent. Together, as though acting on the same instinct, Alexandra and Stefan got out of their chairs to hug me. Victoria joined in, and I sensed a closeness to them I'd never felt before. It was a deep, eternal, unbreakable bond.

I could hear my mother's voice. *Family always comes first. Be grateful for that.*

Letting my kids see me cry was a first for me. Being in the media business for as long as I have been, I've learned that a big part of success is presenting the best possible portrait to your audience, sending the message that everything is fine—in fact, everything is more than fine, it's terrific. When the camera and the microphone are on, you must appear as upbeat, positive, and warm. You have to sound like you're having fun, even if you aren't.

Now it was apparent to all of us that everything *wasn't* fantastic—far from it. I couldn't even try to project confidence, optimism, and good cheer to my kids. Not putting up a front allowed me to connect with them more deeply None of us knew what the outcome would be, but at least we were in it together. I didn't have all the answers, and I couldn't pretend I did. I was deeply grateful for my family at that moment.

From the center of that family hug, I said, "Let's pray."

And we did.

Our Father, who art in Heaven, hallowed be Thy name. Thy kingdom come, Thy will be done, on earth as it is in Heaven. Give us this day our daily bread, and forgive us our trespasses, as we forgive those who trespass against us. And lead us not into temptation but deliver us from evil. Amen.

The Lord's Prayer was the first prayer my mother taught me. I couldn't have been more than three years old. I can't say that prayer or write about it, as I'm doing now, without thinking of her. She used it as her first response to the many hardships she faced. She made a point of telling me many times that she said *The Lord's Prayer* as a young girl during World War II, when her world fell apart. Now it was my world that was falling apart. With my eyes closed, I saw my mother's face as we said, "Thy will be done..." together.

* * *

My family and I had prayed together many times before but never in the face of this kind of adversity. We weren't reciting empty phrases or going through the motions hoping for divine assistance. We were really praying. We were praying for me. We were praying for each other. We were praying for our family, begging God for help. And we hoped our prayers were heard.

Each of the kids said, "I love you, Dad." Then they went back upstairs to their rooms, in silence, uncertainty, and fear.

* * *

Victoria checked me into the hospital on Wednesday, February 3rd. My surgery was scheduled for the following day.

Dr. Girardi came to me in the evening and said, "Stefan, I am really up against the wall energy-wise. Frankly, I'm exhausted. I've done five heart surgeries today, two of which were emergencies—I had no choice. I can still do your surgery tomorrow, but what I'd rather do is get some rest, because what we must do is obviously very serious. It involves a lot of brainpower. I want to make sure that I'm fresh. I know it's going to put you through hell to make you wait, but..."

"Doc," I said, "I hate to interrupt you, but if you think Friday is the right day, then Friday is the right day. Go get some rest!"

He smiled and said, "Okay." He left, and my surgery was moved from Thursday afternoon to Friday morning.

I felt a profound sense of relief and gratitude that Dr. Girardi told me how he was feeling. I was now going to be his first surgery on Friday morning. Even though it meant an extra day of waiting, something told me that being his first patient on Friday, when he was 100 percent fresh, relaxed, and full of energy and focus was part of the plan. All alone in that hospital room, I felt incredibly blessed. If I were going to have that operation, I would have it in the best place, with the best surgeon, and under the best circumstances possible.

In my mind, my mother's voice said, "This is God's will. This is the way He wants it."

* * *

Lying in my hospital bed that long night before the surgery was a surreal experience. I got very little sleep. I was extremely nervous and felt as if there were an atomic bomb waiting to go off within my body, as if the countdown to a cataclysm had begun. Everything in my life was about to change, forever, and there wasn't a damn thing I could do about it.

I still couldn't quite believe this was happening to me. I felt an emptiness, a tremendous sense of the unknown, a feeling of being outside myself, of not living my own life, of watching a movie of someone else's life. Yet here I was, lying in a hospital bed, with the moments passing by every so slowly. This life, whatever was left of it, really was mine.

Victoria and the kids were staying at a friend's apartment nearby. They arrived in my hospital room at 5:45 am. I was wide awake, as I had been for most of the night.

"How you are doing, honey?" Victoria asked.

"Great," I said, but I knew the ragged tone of my voice didn't convey much bravery. All it managed to get across was the reality that I had overdosed on nerves, adrenaline, and insomnia.

✳ ✳ ✳

When the nurses came to get me, we were praying *The Lord's Prayer*. My wife was anointing me with holy water from a small plastic bottle that my mother had given me a few years prior.

We held hands and asked God to protect me, to guide the surgeon and his assistants so that I could have the best possible outcome. Then we stopped holding hands and the nurses wheeled me into the waiting area just outside the operating room. My family followed. We waited there together for a few minutes, which seemed like an eternity, and then, at around 8:00 am, the nurses said it was time for me to go.

I said goodbye to my family and told them all how very much I loved them. Just as the operating room door was opening, I glanced back at my wife and kids, and waved the International Sign Language hand symbol for "I love you": two middle fingers closed, thumb, index, and pinky finger open. They said "I love you," right back using the same gesture. Then the door closed, and they were gone.

The first thing I noticed about the operating room was the cold temperature and incredibly bright lights.

A nurse asked me to get off the gurney so I could get onto the operating table. Before I could get on the operating table, she handed me surgery consent forms. She gave me a summary of what they were going to do and then she asked me to sign the papers. I did. Then I lay down on the table.

As they put the mask over my nose, I remember the anesthesiologist telling me, "Mr. Rybak, I'm going to give you a little something to help you relax."

With the mask on, I thought, *my God, how powerless am I at this moment. I do not control what happens next. I have zero influence. I can't affect the outcome.* There was nothing to do but submit to what was happening to me.

Then I saw my mother's face and thought of God.

My very last thought before I went under was, *Thy will be done.*

CHAPTER
FOUR

Once you lose someone significant, life tends to come at you in fragments, like quick snapshots that flutter through your mind at warp speed.

What follows, in the next part of this book, are the bits and pieces that turned out to be most helpful to me in making sense of my mother's life and death—a task that intensified after my heart scare, a task that turned out to be essential in making sense of my *own* life.

You know by now, of course, that I made it through my heart operation. However, what may not be as clear is how I made it through the complicated reality that awaited me once I woke up in my hospital bed, plugged into a lot of tubes and monitors; how I made it through to making sense of what had just happened to me and was happening to me next; how I made it through to being okay with dying— whenever God chooses that time for me; how I made it through to the idea of putting family first, no matter what.

To make sense of any of that, I had to sift through some of the fragments connected to my mother. Not all of those fragments are pretty. The first one, though, is a beautiful memory.

About a year and nine months before my mother died, I drove to her house in Waterbury, Connecticut. It was my birthday, and the only present I wanted was to be with her. It was snowing hard, but I felt strongly, for some reason, that I needed to just hang out at her house for the day. It was only the two of us, and we watched our two favorite films, *Heaven Can Wait* and *Being There,* two classic movies from the seventies that told stories about destiny and purpose. My mother and I had watched these films together many times before. They were "our" movies.

It was my 54th birthday "party." Just my mother and me. We watched the familiar movie scenes play out as the snow continued to fall. We ate barley soup and sandwiches. My mother's homemade barley soup was the best. She had made that for me because she knew I loved it. We were nestled in comfortably on the couch as we watched our two favorite movies.

There was a sense of total, deep relaxation between the two of us. It was only possible because my mother had just stopped drinking, which was a significant accomplishment, and something she had sworn to me for years she could do at any time she wanted. For most of my life, my mother was a functional alcoholic with a special gift for ruining family gatherings—including events like this one—by getting plastered. Today, she was completely sober, and today, perhaps as a birthday present, she mentioned that she had stopped drinking, forever. "I told you I would do it, Stefan," she said, as we stared at Warren Beatty. "And I did." She turned and smiled at me. Looking back, I know she must have been thinking about all the moments of humiliation, pain, and anger her drinking had caused me and many others.

All of that trauma felt a million miles away now. I was happy just watching movies with my mama on my birthday. I didn't have to worry about any alcohol-fueled problems. That day rests now in my heart as one of the most important moments of my life, right up there with getting married and the birth of my children. I looked at the snow falling and thought, *what an incredible day this is.* No tension. No drinking. No unacceptable behavior. I felt calm, relaxed, comfortable, and safe, in a way I never quite felt as an adult before. There was just a deep bond between the two of us, and there was no one else around to screw it up. There was no alcohol to darken the day.

In a way, I felt as if my mother was asking for my forgiveness for her many years of abusive drinking—but my mother, the proud and stubborn woman she was, never put that apology into words. Sitting down, being together, and watching a movie with me was probably as close as she could ever get to saying, *I'm sorry.* If that's what my mother was saying, I heard her and forgave her in that very moment.

CHAPTER
FIVE

One of the big lessons I've learned since my operation is that what I don't know about my mother's life is often just as relevant and vital as what I do know. I've learned a lot from the facts I know for certain about her, but I've also learned a lot from the gaps. And sometimes, I've learned the most from things that she chose not to tell me.

It's as if my mother's long life was like a giant, complicated jigsaw puzzle, with a significant number of missing and broken pieces—very frustrating. I wondered, as I tried to put the puzzle together, whether some pieces were thrown away on purpose. Perhaps all lives are like that—incomplete jigsaw puzzles left behind. We cannot expect the living to fill in all the gaps.

No matter how much I think about my mother's life, no matter how carefully I review the bits and pieces of near and distant memories, the picture that emerges is not clear or definitive. It has many empty spots where the viewer must fill in the details. The portrait that emerges is a mixture of saint and sinner, of a very human person, someone who made mistakes, but who also found a way to grow stronger in adversity, someone who did not lose her faith in God, even in the face of hardship, death, and disaster. It's a picture that has become much more important to me since I had my own brushes with such realities and since I realized that my mother was a survivor of what would today be called Post-Traumatic Stress Syndrome. Despite its many defects, hers is a picture worth saving and cherishing, which is why I decided to write this book.

My mother's information that shows up in these pages comes from my personal experiences with her and from things she said to my siblings and me as we were growing up. This information is not the whole woman, but it's all the pieces of the puzzle I could find.

My mother, Maria Olszak, was born on August 13, 1925, and raised in southeastern Poland, near a town called Sporniak. When Hitler invaded Poland on September 1, 1939, my mother had just turned 14 years old. She grew up in a farming family and was a good student who worked hard to achieve good grades. She liked being with people but enjoyed private moments of thought and reflection.

My mother was sitting alone in a field one day, doing her homework, when she heard a loud noise in the sky.

When she looked up in the distance, she saw a group of airplanes approaching; then she saw what looked like silver balls falling from the planes. It was the German Air Force bombing the town. My mother gathered up her books and raced toward home. We don't know what my mother said to her parents, or anyone else, about what she'd seen. We don't know what her family did when the town was bombed and invaded by the Germans.

* * *

There is a gap in her life story now of about a year and a half. The next puzzle piece is well into the war, sometime in the latter half of 1941.

One day, at the age of 16, my mother was walking to school when a gang of men wearing swastikas intercepted her before she could get there. She was kidnapped, along with many other young people, by Nazi forces. They took all the Polish youth they could find. The German army wanted to put them all to work.

My mother never discussed the details of her capture. She did not tell us who captured her or how she felt when it happened.

My mother did tell my sister, Barbara, that she was shipped by train to a labor camp somewhere in Germany. She was one of many thousands of Poles who slaved in unwilling support of the Nazi war effort.

This part of the story, the part about her being kidnapped on the way to school and sent to a labor camp, only became apparent to me during a discussion that I had with Barbara. I felt a strange mixture of emotions when I heard it. Pride in the idea that my mother could survive being sent to such a place, and shock that she had been exposed to it. I even felt a twinge of resentment that she could keep something that important from me. Maybe, in her own way, my mother was trying to protect me from this horror; after all, I was her youngest of six children, and she always referred to me as her baby, even after I became an adult. In my mother's eyes, I suppose that I was more vulnerable and more deserving of protection from the most brutal facts. The truth is that my mother didn't like talking much about the horrors that World War II brought into her life. I'm sharing the moments that my siblings and I pieced together, over decades, from various discussions about what happened to her during the war. Her answers to those questions were typically not very long or detailed. It wasn't something she wanted to focus on or think about.

My mother saw pregnant women getting kicked in the stomach by Nazi officers wearing heavy leather boots at the labor camp. She saw those women dragged away to rooms where more torture awaited them. She could hardly imagine what would then happen to them, and she didn't want to think about it. She saw the terrible abuse of women and children by Nazi officers. She saw children knocked to the ground and pulled around by their hair. When she was pressed for details about what else she'd seen, she'd grow quiet and act as if she'd already said too much. It was as though she had made a mistake answering the question in the first place.

When we lived in Connecticut in the early 1960s, my sister, Barbara, who was 12 or 13 years old at the time, saw our mother play host to a group of seven or eight women she called "The Rabbits." It was a strange name for these women, and reflected a strange common bond with my mother. They were women who, as young students, had been part of the Polish underground resistance, intent on defying the brutal Nazi regime. Captured by the Gestapo, they were sent to Ravensbrück, the concentration camp known as "Hitler's Hell for Women." This is where my mother was also sent.

They were called "The Rabbits" because the Third Reich used them as laboratory animals for medical experiments. The Nazis had used their limbs to simulate war wounds; they infected those wounds with aggressive bacteria, wood chips, and glass, trying to cause gangrene, which they would then attempt to treat. They also experimented with removing and damaging nerves, muscles, and even bones in the legs. They limped; their legs lacked any muscle and had deep indentations from surgical removal of bone and tendons.

Some of the women who survived knew my mother. Barbara recalls that my mother would have these ladies over for dinner. They made a point of telling Barbara their stories in the hope that they wouldn't be forgotten. Barbara doesn't remember all of the details. She does recall that "The Rabbits" were as forthcoming as my mother was circumspect. One of these women showed Barbara her bare leg. There was a horrible scar where someone had taken away the muscle.

At the time of these discussions, I was an infant. I didn't learn about what went on in Ravensbrück until many years later, after my mother's death. I can understand the decision to withhold this painful information from a young child. But my mother and I connected as adults, too. She and I had decades to talk about this. Somehow, she never got around to it, though I asked my fair share of questions about what had happened during this period. What led her to compartmentalize this corner of her life and keep me from ever being a part of it? I will never know for sure.

So far as Barbara and I know, my mother avoided being subjected to medical experiments. We don't know how she managed that. She may have been considered too young for such barbarity, but that seems unlikely. The Nazi doctors didn't seem to have been all that picky. Perhaps she worked very hard. She was young and healthy. Maybe there was a system under which hard workers were spared that treatment. There may be some other explanation. In any event, we know she was surrounded by this mayhem, this inhumanity, and we know she worked long hours in the labor camp at the age of 16. We know she saw things no 16-year-old should have seen. We don't know what kind of work she did there. We know her youth was over too soon. We know it was stolen from her. We know her real job was to survive.

✶ ✶ ✶

When pressed for specifics on what she had gone through during these years, my mother, as I recall, only responded with generalities. She told us that she always prayed to God that she would find a way to escape all the difficulties that she faced during the war. She said her family was religious, and they all prayed for survival.

We don't know when my mother got out of the labor camp. Even though she never told us, Barbara and I feel sure, based on our knowledge of her character, that she decided to get out and took some kind of action.

CHAPTER
SIX

Whatever means my mother took to get out of Ravensbrück, she did so because she was a strong-willed person. I had so many experiences of seeing her in action, pursuing something she wanted, that I couldn't imagine her passively accepting her fate in such a horrific environment. She must have taken *some* action, had *some* plan. But whenever I would ask her about such things, I'd get annoying-vague responses like, "Stefan, that was such a long time ago," or, "Who can remember?"

According to my sister, Barbara, our mother said she went out of her way to erase most of her memories about that time. When Barbara asked for details, she would push back by saying things like, "I made up my mind to survive, and did everything I could. Most of all, I prayed and prayed to God. That's all I remember."

I only came to realize after her death that my mother had actively chosen not to remember certain aspects of her life, perhaps as a coping skill to deal with the various forms of the war-related trauma that she encountered. Forgetting was a big part of how she survived. As it turned out, there was a lot to forget. Her whole life was, to a significant degree, measured out in trauma.

Barbara said our mother got through her time in the Nazi labor camp because she knew God would be by her side. She willed herself to survive, and her number one survival mechanism was constant prayer. My mother had a sincere belief that God had a purpose for her life, and that, somehow, God would allow her to survive to fulfill that purpose.

That's all very obscure, of course. We know for sure that there came a day when a German officer selected my mother to serve as his maid and personal assistant. Upon winning this job, she was allowed to leave the labor camp and live in a cramped attic room of this officer's home.

Her new job was actually considered to be a plum assignment, and there must have been a great deal of competition for it. We have no idea how she first heard about this "escape" from the labor camp, what the selection process was for selecting such workers, or what my mother might have done at the time to take advantage of it. Perhaps it was an answered prayer. Her life could be measured out in those, too.

We figure that my mother must have been around 17 years old when the officer selected her to work at his home. She had probably spent about nine months in Ravensbrück.

When the German officer (whose name we will never know, but whom my mother called simply "the general") first came in contact with her, he would have noticed several advantages she brought to the position he needed to fill. My mother was young, healthy, and active. In addition to Polish, my mother spoke German and English, having studied these languages in school. My mother was bold, diligent, and purposeful. The photographs of my mother during this period show that she was also strikingly beautiful. Barbara and I agreed that it was probably a combination of all of these qualities that got her the job.

My mother was able to walk out of the labor camp alive, with her limbs, faculties, and at least some portion of her dignity intact, which is something many people who entered Ravensbrück were not able to do. She told Barbara that the general was kind to her and did not take advantage of her in any sexual way.

* * *

Maybe the general liked the idea of a nice-looking young woman working around the house. I suppose it's as easy to imagine that reality for her, as a 17-year-old kidnapped victim, as it is to believe any other. The only obstacle to it, I suppose, is the challenge I have of picturing a Nazi general showing kindness to someone attractive, indebted to him for her survival, and utterly under his control. But when you are putting together a jigsaw puzzle, you must find a way to leave the blank spaces blank, not fixate on them too much, and perhaps even show some gratitude for what you do not know and may never know. I choose to picture the general, Nazi or not, as someone with a shred of honor, and as someone who decided to show this woman, who would one day become my mother, some kindness rather than to exploit her. But it takes an effort of will for me to do that. I'm willing to make that effort.

The attic room my mother lived in at the general's house had a low ceiling. It was freezing in the winter, and my mother shivered in the cold darkness of those nights. She told Barbara that she often dreamt of her father coming to visit, warming her up, comforting her, and praying with her. She said that the dreams were sometimes so vivid and lifelike that she often had difficulty distinguishing them from reality.

Perhaps her father, far away, back in Poland, really was trying to reach out to her during these agonizing nights. Maybe these visions or dreams provided some kind of connection between the two. We do know, as my mother grew up, they were very close.

I've thought of those attic visions of my mother's often as I worked on this book. I have no idea whether people really can connect from such a distance. I don't think there can be any final answer to such a question. Sometimes I have pictured myself as the one in the attic, the one shivering in an unfamiliar bed. I imagine my mother visiting to comfort me, to remind me of her presence and her love, to encourage me to keep going, to keep praying, to keep trusting that the right path forward will eventually reveal itself for me. I picture her vividly, aiming to make up for all the times she wasn't able to be there for me in person. I like to tell myself that such connections across vast distances of space and time and choices, across even the bridge that divides the realms of the living and the dead, are possible.

CHAPTER
SEVEN

The more closely I look at my mother's life and reflect on my own, the more I believe that she was fated to deal with long, ongoing wars. Some of her battles show up in the history books—but not all of them. I don't know if my mother was ever able to move past her battles.

What follows is my piecing together the balance of my mother's time during one war in particular—World War II.

My mother said that the general was very kind to her, but that his wife, whom she always called *The Bitch*, was quite another story.

The Bitch worked my mother like a slave, which I suppose she was. While the Bitch slept, my mother would get up very early and make sure the table was set, and the car was ready for the general. She would serve the general his coffee and breakfast and stand at attention until he left for work. By this point, the Bitch was awake, and it seems as though my mother was obliged to serve her as well. Once that was attended to, the real workday would begin.

The Bitch delighted in tormenting my mother once the general was out of the house. For instance, she would order my mother to wash the same floor, over and over again, all the while standing over her, staring, glaring, and making derogatory comments about Polish people and about how utterly worthless she thought my mother was. The Bitch also derisively told my mother that she'd never amount to anything and being a slave would be the best thing she'd ever do in her life. This sounds like pure sadism, and from the venom that entered my mother's voice every time she spoke of this woman, it's hard for me to classify it as anything else.

The same do-it-again, stand-and-stare routine appears to have played out each working day, and every time the general left the house. My mother washed the dishes, cleaned the clothes, and did other housekeeping and manual labor. The Bitch, my mother said, specialized in telling her what a terrible job she had been doing. To hear my mother tell it, this is what the Bitch lived for, day after endless day. It must have been a horrible life.

My mother told us that she prayed for her safety, well-being, and freedom every night on her knees, up in that cold, musty, tiny attic. One day, in 1945, my mother's prayers were finally answered. The Allies liberated the area. A group of American soldiers came in and commandeered the house. The officer-in-charge ordered the General, the General's wife, and my mother out of the house. He brought them outside and, speaking German, made the general and his wife identify themselves. They did. Then he asked my mother who she was.

My mother gave him her name and told him how long she had been in forced labor, both in the camp and in this general's house. She said she was incredibly thankful to the Americans for coming in to rescue her. She said she had been praying for that. She asked the American who was in charge to be very kind to the general.

"He always treated me with respect," she said. "He did nothing to hurt me, ever. He is a kind man." She then pointed at the German general's wife and said, "But you can hang that bitch from the nearest tree."

I have no idea what expression passed over that sadistic woman's face as my mother spoke these words, but today I imagine it as the expression of an evil person realizing she's been cornered, at last. Out of all the strange things that happened to my mom, for some reason her abuse at the hands of this woman stands out as the most unforgivable— but perhaps that's because this particular memory is the one she chose to share with me.

The American officer asked her if there were any valuables in the house. My mother looked at the general, and he bowed his head. It was a sign of understanding that he knew she had to do this. She had to show the Americans what they wanted to see. She knew where all the valuables were, so she led the Americans to everything. The last thing she showed them was the general's stock of wine. He kept it in the lake nearby. He liked to keep the wine cold.

The Americans took the wine and everything else. As far as we can make out, they didn't hang the general or his wife. They brought my mother to a resettlement camp.

I'd like to be able to say that the war ended for my mother that day, but it was only a continuation of a long series of battles that scarred my mother's life. That day was the beginning of a whole new trail of battles, in a long-running war that never made it into the history books: a war of love and hate, man and woman, father and child.

In such wars, I have learned, happy endings are not always to be expected.

CHAPTER
EIGHT

There's a passage in the Gospel of Mark (5:11) that reads:

Blessed are you when they revile and persecute you and say all kinds of evil against you falsely for My sake. Rejoice and be exceedingly glad, for great is your reward in heaven, for so they persecuted the prophets who were before you.

Later in the same chapter (5:39-40), this follows:

If anyone slaps you on the right cheek, turn to them the other cheek also. And if anyone wants to sue you and take your shirt, hand over your coat as well.

These verses can be difficult to understand and hard to live with for anyone who grew up, as I did, in an abusive household. From a distance, they might seem to be arguing for complete capitulation to the experience of being attacked and victimized—but I've known for years now that that's not what Jesus had in mind when he spoke these words. These passages now seem to me to have much more in common with Zen Koans—the classic teaching riddles of Buddhism that delight in presenting a seemingly impossible paradox such as, *What is the sound of one hand clapping?* Such a riddle helps move the student beyond the realm of rational thought and into a more in-depth direct experience of spirituality.

I mention these Bible verses because it's taken me several dozen years to realize that they were pointing me toward a better understanding of my relationship with my father. As I read them now, I wonder what my mother made of them. I never found out. But I can share what I have come to make of them with you, and I can imagine her agreeing with me. I believe these verses reconnect us to the core concept of The Lord's Prayer: *Thy will be done.*

Thy will be done doesn't mean you give up the responsibility to make good choices. It doesn't expect you to stay in a situation where you're being abused. It means you accept whatever is in front of you with sincere gratitude, as God's will; you put it in perspective; you learn what you can from it; and you go from there wiser and more astute, without perpetuating a downward cycle. Along the way, if there's been suffering, you look for ways to put that in perspective, too. You accept that there's a plan that is bigger and better than you could possibly and rationally understand. And you find a way to rejoice in the life God has granted to you, on the road He's given you to walk, wherever that road leads.

My father, Tadeusz Jan Rybak, was born April 21, 1916, in Warsaw, Poland. Unfortunately, we know a good deal less about his life than my mother's. He was a very handsome man who, during his life, walked, for reasons known best to God, a painful road.

My father was an officer in the Polish army. I don't know exactly when he started his training, but I know he attended a military academy similar to West Point. The army was my father's career, and he fought against the Nazis when they invaded Poland.

In 1939, when my father was 23 years old, he was involved in a battle with the Nazis. This would have been near the start of World War II. He was wounded in the wrist and the knee. Hobbled by these injuries, he was taken a prisoner and placed in a German prisoner of war camp for over five and half years.

There is one more thing I know about my father's service during World War II; he shared this story with me on several occasions. The guards at the prisoner of war camp where he was being held had a sick, sadistic sense of humor, and they took particular pleasure in playing Russian roulette with the inmates.

One of the guards would go into the cell where my dad and the other prisoners were held, place a pistol or rifle at the skull of one of the occupants, and pull the trigger. The prisoners learned how the game worked pretty fast. Sometimes there would be a bullet in the chamber, and sometimes there wouldn't. The whole point was, you never knew whether you were being executed or not, and neither did the men who shared the cell with you. Not even the guard knew.

I remember my father telling me that he and a few other men were in his cell one day; he was shaving. He had a little mirror set up over the sink, and he was looking into the mirror with great care to make sure he didn't cut himself when he heard the cell door open. In the mirror, he caught a glimpse of a guard walking toward him with what one had to assume was a loaded rifle. My dad felt the barrel of the gun against the back of his head. He thought to himself, *This is it. This is the moment I'm going to die.* He shut his eyes. Then he heard a little click—no bullet. He listened to the Nazi laugh a deep, strange laugh, and then he heard the cell door slam. When he finally opened his eyes, he saw his face, half-covered with shaving cream. He couldn't finish shaving because his hands were shaking uncontrollably.

And that's it. That's all we know. Many years after my father shared that story with me, I saw the film *The Deer Hunter,* which features several harrowing scenes of American servicemen forced to play Russian Roulette with their captors during the Vietnam War. Even though it dealt with Vietnam, I was disturbed by the film because I knew it applied to a lot of what my father had gone through during World War II. It also applied to my mother, to a certain extent, if you look at the Russian Roulette game as a metaphor for lethal, unpredictable outbursts of madness and mayhem. They both had to deal with that.

It's a little frustrating that I don't know anything else about my father's experiences during World War II. What I do know, though, is that, after the liberation of Europe, he was resettled to a new camp for refugees, a place where people weren't in danger of having their brains blown out. It was while he was in that camp—a place where men could come and go pretty much as they pleased— that he first saw my mother.

She was on an errand, riding a bicycle past a field near the camp. The man who was to be my father noticed this beautiful, young woman, called out to her, and hoped she would stop pedaling for a moment and talk to him. His voice, she recalled, sounded a bit harsh.

I remember times when my father would sit in the living room, staring straight ahead, not saying a word. You could tell from the expression on his face and the posture of his body, that he was a furious man—so mad at so many things for so long that he was now unable to stop being angry. That was his default setting. That was the father I knew. I suppose, if I had gone through what he had gone through, I would be angry too.

Suffice it to say for now that it's only in recent years, and notably during the process of writing this book, that I have begun to develop a personal understanding of what my father must have endured in the years before his wife and kids came along. I have an understanding of why he behaved the way he did when he was around us. I knew that he was a troubled man. What I have only just now come to understand is that someone doesn't survive a game like the one he survived without becoming one's own walking, talking game of Russian Roulette—someone likely to explode at any moment, for no apparent reason, and with devastating consequences.

With the distance of time, and with the objectivity necessary to write this book, I've discovered an entirely different way of looking at my father than the way I viewed him when I was a younger man. I've come to look at him, not as one of the pivot points of the universe, but to look at him as someone with his own life to live and his own part to play; as a human being with his private road to travel, a path very different from my own and yet intersecting with it. Those roads intertwined, not in ways he designed, not in ways I created, but in ways God ordained. Yes, there were blessings in that journey for both of us, though we didn't always realize them at the time. However, I am grateful for the journey now.

I don't know if he ever got to the point of acceptance in his own life of *Thy will be done.* I know now that he was part of a bigger, better plan than either of us realized while he was here—a divine plan. I picture my mother pedaling her bicycle and trying to decide whether or not she should stop and talk to the man with the harsh voice.

CHAPTER
NINE

We're not exactly sure where my parents stayed or what they did to get by in the years immediately following their marriage—a marriage compelled by my mother's pregnancy. What we do know is that they started a family amid a devastated, shattered Europe, a continent whose infrastructure, social arrangements, and economic base had been pounded to dust by the raging armies and air assaults of World War II.

The entire continent was in chaos. It had not yet been lifted by the Marshall Plan, that massive infusion of cash and goodwill of the United States that kicked in around the middle of 1948. In the three desperate years before that large American aid package materialized, Europe hovered on the brink of starvation. Privation and instability were everywhere, and somehow my parents managed not only to struggle through this time of scarcity, but to bring not one, but two children into the world and keep them safe. How they managed is something my mother didn't discuss.

We know something else about this period, or we can at least infer from the events that followed. My parents harbored a dream of going to America.

It's a measure of how desperate things must have been for them that they leaped at the chance to emigrate to the United States when they heard talk of refugee settlement programs. They put considerable time and effort into the then-essential task of securing an American sponsor who would care for them and facilitate their transition to American life. Setting this up was no easy task since they were refugees and not rich. They knew no one in the faraway, impossibly vast country where they wanted to live. I picture my mother praying for a sponsor and for the means to make the journey. I'm sure she also prayed to God for a safe passage to the United States. Indeed, I have every reason to believe she *must* have prayed for these things.

I know my mother must have known that the journey she was contemplating was not going to be an easy one because she was pregnant with her third child by the time the applications were made. That she even agreed to undertake such an odyssey with a husband and two small children in tow, and pregnant, suggests to me that her life must have been genuinely miserable where she was.

It seems evident that my mother decided that raising a family in the chaos and squalor of post-war Europe was simply unacceptable. I feel certain she saw the escape to the United States as an essential and perhaps even non-negotiable event for herself and her family. Just as she had set her mind on escaping the labor camp and surviving the war, she put her mind now on going to America.

My mother prayed for God's support in all that she wanted in life. She didn't always get what she wanted. None of us do. But my mother sought it with the kind of unstoppable persistence that made you feel sorry you got up in the morning if you happened to be the one who stood in her way. She had a habit of making sure you knew she was going to get what she was after.

When my mother decided that she wanted a life in the United States of America, she went for it. Back in the 1940s, that meant scraping together the money for an ocean voyage or arranging for someone else to pay for it. Since my family consisted of four impoverished war refugees, with another one on the way, it also meant that the American sponsor who emerged would have to be trusted with everything, on faith. This individual would have a significant impact on the American life that eventually emerged for my mother, her husband, and her children.

In this case, the sponsor, secured through some refugee placement service or another, turned out to be a Mississippi cotton farmer. My dad signed on to pick cotton for him. The little family sailed for New Orleans.

What that long, exhausting, and uncomfortable ocean voyage would have been like for a pregnant woman, I don't know. What I do know is that when the journey was complete, the refugees caught a bus from New Orleans for a bumpy journey to some now-forgotten Mississippi town. There, they started their new life in their new country.

If they had ever imagined the wealthy cities and cosmopolitan surroundings of popular movies as the *America* they were coming to live in. I suspect that long drive along the poorly maintained highways of the impoverished states of the Deep South must have disabused them of any romantic notions. This was a hardscrabble existence they had signed on for. It must have been a sobering trip.

It's impossible to say whether my mother and dad knew, when they started that ocean voyage, just how low a Mississippi cotton-picker ranked on the American economic and social scale. However, something tells me that even if they had known, they'd have made the trip. If they had any better options, they would certainly have taken advantage of them.

This next part of her life, my mother did occasionally talk about. She loathed Mississippi. It was hot and humid, and the farmer was a glum and dour man who was deeply skeptical of Catholics. My dad's working hours were long, and his mood was usually sour. The little shack that the four of them lived in was primitive. Rural Mississippi may have been better than where they had just come from, but my mother told us many times that she knew right away Mississippi was not where she wanted to give birth to her third child.

My mother told us that she thanked God every day for the safe passage from Europe once she arrived in America. And she also prayed for another safe passage out of Mississippi before the next baby came.

56

CHAPTER
TEN

My parents must have been grateful for the opportunity to leave ravaged, war-torn Europe, and equally grateful for arriving safely in the United States with their two young children. I'm sure, too, though, that neither of them felt living on a cotton farm in rural Mississippi could ever be the fulfillment of their best hopes and fondest dreams. My father, a proud military man, found himself working the long and unrewarding hours of a cotton picker. My mother had another baby on the way, and she was sweltering in a tiny shack in the middle of nowhere, built over a pigpen, with newspaper covering the interior walls and no running water or electricity. They were both on the lookout for someplace better to settle their young family. A dirty, dusty, pig-infested cotton farm in Mississippi, wasn't it. As I've already said, she was praying for a better place to call home before baby number three showed up.

The answer to that prayer came in the form of a letter from a Mr. Gebalski, one of my father's Polish war buddies, who had temporarily settled in Massachusetts with his wife and child. I have no idea how he managed to get in touch with my father all the way down in Mississippi. The contents of the letter equated roughly to, "There's work up here in Lynn, Massachusetts; move up here with your family, and I'll help you get a job and get settled."

Apparently, it didn't take my parents long to decide to take my father's military friend up on this offer because they arrived in Massachusetts in early 1950. After getting to Mississippi in September 1949, it seems that they stayed there for about five or six months and then made their way to Massachusetts as soon as the opportunity presented itself. That meant embarking on yet another long, uncomfortable journey.

Since they didn't have enough money to take a train, they traveled from Mississippi to Massachusetts on a bus. I imagine my parents and their two young children, Barbara and Andrew, crammed into some old Greyhound, making the arduous, 1400-mile journey, which, back then, would have taken two or three days, maybe even longer. Since the Interstate Highway System hadn't been built yet, they probably traveled on poorly maintained two-lane roads and bumpy back streets. At this time, my mother would have been about seven or eight months pregnant.

It was the promise of a job in a factory for my father that drew them to Lynn, but as it happened that employment didn't materialize. To support his family, my father took a job as a garbage man. Then, in April 1950, my sister Jane was born.

Jane's birth presented yet another major challenge for my mother. When she first laid eyes on her newborn baby, my mother said that Jane's skin appeared to be blue. The doctors and nurses said that upon birth, Jane had a hard time breathing. As time went on, it was clear that Jane was not like other children. She was labeled as being mentally retarded. In later years, her condition was diagnosed as cerebral palsy. Nowadays, we'd say she was developmentally disabled. Regardless of the label one applies to her situation, it was the latest in a series of setbacks that might well have devastated another family.

It's important to bear in mind that, back in the 1950s, the attitude toward people with mental disabilities was very different. People who were "retarded" were considered an embarrassment to the family and a scourge on society. Certainly, there must have been pressure put on my parents by doctors, nurses, perhaps even a social worker, to have Jane permanently institutionalized to spare the family the "shame" of raising her. I'm sure they must have suggested locking her up in a facility with others more like her—to keep her away from "normal people."

My mother told us many times that she never considered such an option. She chose to give Jane the care and support she needed. She was her daughter and of her own flesh and blood. This choice would have a tremendous and long-lasting impact on my parents' marriage, and our family dynamic. My mother chose to see Jane's disability as part of her own journey, part of the larger plan of God's will. I believe this was how she looked at every strange, seemingly random twist of fate that came her way. I know it was how she looked at this one because I vividly remember her describing it in such terms.

My mother had a great deal of experience dealing with what others would call bad luck, and she never missed an opportunity to talk about these experiences. All were opportunities to draw closer to God. At moments of difficulty in my own life, my mother would say, "Stefan, always depend on God. He is your friend." She would also say, "Go to God for everything and trust His answer. Even if you don't understand the answer God gives you, understand that it is still the answer. Although you may not like it or understand it, God's answer is always the best answer."

I want you to understand this was a life principle that my mother lived by: *God's answer is always the best answer.* It wasn't just a lecture she gave me or a set of nice-sounding philosophical slogans she passed along. It was how my mother lived. For her, it was "God's will be done," in action, every day. From my mother's perspective, the same God, who answered her prayers to get out of the labor camp, to escape imprisonment and slave labor, travel to America, and make it out of Mississippi, had given her a job. That job was to take care of her children and to do her utmost to keep them safe and loved, including, and especially, Jane. My mother didn't deviate from that.

CHAPTER
ELEVEN

In the years before I was born, my parents' relationship had already begun a long, slow, and unstoppable period of deterioration.

After they made it from Mississippi to New England, the glue called "survive the aftermath of World War II and get to America," which seemed to hold them together fairly well up to that point, started to crack and weaken. Jane's birth and her needs as a developmentally disabled child added other cracks. Given what I've shared with you about my parents' war experience, it should come as no surprise that they were both dealing with Post-Traumatic Stress Disorder. What I think may be surprising, though, is the way my mother responded to the slow-motion train wreck that was her marriage.

The worse my mother's relationship with my father got—and believe me, it got terrible—with his pursuing a series of girlfriends, subjecting us to violence at home, moving out, and eventually leaving my mother to fend for herself and all of us, without a penny in child support—the more emotionally reliant she became on her relationship with Jane.

My mother allowed Jane to become utterly dependent upon her. She saw this dependence as protecting Jane. But I can see now that it wasn't just that. Somehow, my mother was protecting herself as well.

By the time I came along in 1958, Jane was eight years old; but because she had cerebral palsy, she was still being tended to as though she were a toddler. This was strange, at least from a modern perspective, because we now know that kids with cerebral palsy have varying degrees of physical disability. Some have only mild impairment, while others are severely affected.

Looking back now, I realize that Jane's condition was nowhere near the most extreme end of the scale. Yet as my parents' relationship collapsed, my mother acted as though Jane was at the far end of the disability scale. Jane's cerebral palsy had left her with an obstacle to overcome, but it had not left her completely helpless. Jane could indeed learn simple tasks like making a sandwich and tying her shoes, but my mother eventually chose to do all of these things, and much more, for her.

Here is the hard truth. The further my mother got away from my father emotionally, the more she kept Jane from learning how to do things for herself. As Jane moved through her adolescence and into her young adulthood, she found herself tended to by a mother whose main goal was to keep her from mastering basic life skills that could have made her more independent.

The reason for this, I think, is straightforward. The more obvious it became to my mother that my father didn't love her enough to change his way of living—to stop philandering, for instance, or to stop abusing his wife and children—the more convinced she became that he didn't need her. It became very important for my mother to have someone in her life who not only *did* need her, but who would never *stop* needing her. That someone was Jane.

As a result, Jane became overly dependent on my mother. Jane was a young woman in her early twenties who had been taught zero self-reliance when my parents finally split for good in the early '70s; I was still in grade school. Jane's complete and absolute reliance on my mother meant she didn't establish a desire to grow or to expand or try to make the most of her own capacities. This was something Barbara and I knew was not good for her or our mother. But it was what our family looked like. My mother was a working mom who, after about 1971, had two full-time jobs, one of which was doing everything for Jane. It was not a healthy situation.

I was only a young teenager during these years, and I certainly wasn't up for challenging my mother on such a point. Barbara, though, was older and far more prepared for that conversation than I was, and one day she did confront my mother about it.

Over dinner, she told my mother that she thought Jane would do a lot better if she let her learn and experiment more, even if it meant failing at times. She told my mother that there were lots of things Jane could be learning but wasn't. Barbara made the point that having cerebral palsy didn't automatically mean that someone was utterly incapable of learning to care for herself. It meant that the person had a different set of abilities than most other people. The only way we would understand what Jane was truly capable of was to back off a little bit and let her try to do things on her own. Barbara didn't want Jane to spend her entire life being cared for as though she was a potted plant. Barbara argued forcefully with my mother to let Jane become a bit more independent. *What would happen when my mother was too old to care for Jane?* It was a good question, I thought. I'll never forget my mother's response.

My mother said, "God forbid that you or your brother should ever have a handicapped child, Barbara." She must have sensed where my sympathies aligned in this discussion, although I hadn't said a word. "Until you do, you'll never understand, either of you. So don't try to pretend that you do."

I remember thinking that Barbara was right, that my mother had been wrong in dismissing her concerns, and that Jane was indeed on the receiving end of too much of my mother's attention. I remember thinking that my mother was playing a special card to end that discussion. Barbara and I didn't know what it was like to have a disabled child. My mother did. We had no say in the matter. It seemed deeply manipulative to shut down the exchange in that way, and perhaps it was.

Looking back now, though, I think I can understand a little better than I did at the time why my mother was not only fiercely protective of Jane but also intensely protective of the *way* she cared for her. It's human nature to want to be needed. My mother had a difficult life, and her husband was gone, and perhaps she had a right to compensate for some of those difficulties in the way that seemed best for her. In any event, she and Jane gave each other a sense of purpose. Who was I to begrudge either of them?

Love had come to my mother through Jane. Unconditional, unvarying, unstoppable, impossible-to-betray love. I see now that even though she made choices I would not have made, she had also gone through things I cannot imagine. Perhaps she was entitled to that kind of love, on whatever terms she chose to sustain it. Maybe, for her, that kind of love was a gift from God.

This is one of my favorite photos of my mother. I'm guessing it's sometime during the 1950s. She's in her late 20s/early 30s, dressed up fancy, and looking so beautiful and happy.

My mother and me, Christmas Eve, 2010.

*My mother and me, backstage with Johnny Mathis,
one of her favorite singers. This was the Summer of
1995, around the time of my mother's 70th birthday,
at the Oakdale Theatre in Wallingford, Connecticut.*

*August 13, 2013, my mother and me on her 88th birthday.
Lymphoma would claim her life two months later.*

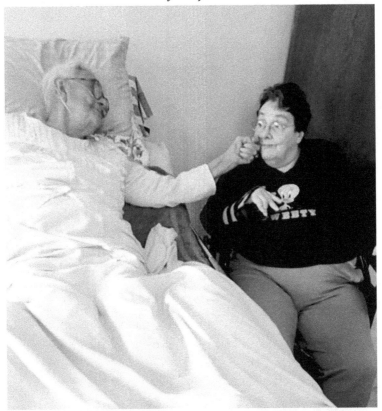

This photo was taken three days before my mother died. With her health failing fast, my mother wanted to see Jane one final time. We were able to have Jane transported from the nursing home that she resided in then to my mother's home. The loving caress of Jane's cheek speaks to the tender love these two shared for each other.

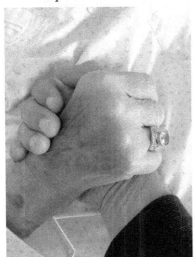

My mother and I holding hands as she lay in her bed, at home, in a coma, heading toward death, which would occur less than 24 hours later (from the back cover).

My dad and sister Barbara, in Germany, circa 1947.

This photo was taken circa 1948. It's my father, mother, and sister Barbara in Germany, about a year before they came to America.

My father and me, circa 1970.

My mother and my sister Jane, circa 1970.

*My senior yearbook photo from Holy Cross
High School in Waterbury, Connecticut, 1976.*

*Me in the summer of 1976 between high school
graduation and starting college that Fall.*

March 1978, broadcasting live on WWCO radio in my hometown of Waterbury, Connecticut. We were collecting food and monetary donations for a local food bank.

Me on the air on WWCO radio, 1978. I was 20 years old, it was my second year as a professional disc jockey, and I was having the time of my life.

Me on the cover of "Hitmakers" magazine, April 1990. This gave me national exposure in the radio and records industry, and led to excellent professional opportunities.

WWCO • 1240

WEEK OF SEPTEMBER 26, 1977

LW / TW		TITLE	ARTIST
2	1	THAT'S ROCK N' ROLL	SHAUN CASSIDY
4	2	STAR WARS	MECO
3	3	KEEP IT COMIN' LOVE	KC/SUNSHINE
5	4	STRAWBERRY LETTER #23	BROTHERS JOHNSON
6	5	NOBODY DOES IT BETTER	CARLY SIMON
7	6	ON AND ON	STEPHEN BISHOP
8	7	SWAYING TO THE MUSIC	JOHNNY RIVERS
12	8	BOOGIE NIGHTS	HEATWAVE
1	9	DON'T STOP	FLEETWOOD MAC
16	10	YOU LIGHT UP MY LIFE	DEBBY BOONE
13	11	COLD AS ICE	FOREIGNER
15	12	JUNGLE LOVE	STEVE MILLER
17	13	WAY DOWN	ELVIS
19	14	THEME: "ONE ON ONE"	SEALS & CROFTS
18	15	DON'T WORRY BABY	B. J. THOMAS
9	16	TELEPHONE LINE	ELO
20	17	I FEEL LOVE	DONNA SUMMER
23	18	BRICKHOUSE	COMMODORES
21	19	SIGNED,SEALED,DELIVERED	PETER FRAMPTON
11	20	BEST OF MY LOVE	EMOTIONS
22	21	HEAVEN ON THE 7TH FLOOR	PAUL NICHOLAS
14	22	FLOAT ON	FLOATERS
25	23	SHOOP SHOOP SONG	KATE TAYLOR
NM	24	THE KING IS GONE	RONNIE McDOWELL
26	25	SURFIN' U.S.A.	LEIF GARRETT
27	26	SHE DID IT	ERIC CARMEN
29	27	IT WAS ALMOST LIKE A SONG	RONNIE MILSAP
10	28	SMOKE FROM A DISTANT FIRE	SANFORD/TOWNSEND
NM	29	ANOTHER STAR	STEVIE WONDER
NM	30	JUST REMEMBER I LOVE YOU	FIREFALL

STEF RYBAK...."IN THE NIGHT-TIME" WITH
WATERBURY'S BEST MUSIC...ON SUPER MUSIC C-O

NEW MUSIC

HELP IS ON ITS WAY	LITTLE RIVER
DAYTIME FRIENDS	KENNY ROGERS
MY BROWN EYES BLUE	CRYSTAL GAYLE
DAYBREAK	BARRY MANILOW
BABY,WHAT A SURPRISE	CHICAGO
WE'RE ALL ALONE	RITA COOLIDGE

T-M MUSIC SCENE   SEE OTHER SIDE ▶

The Top 30 songs on WWCO radio, plus the new songs that were added for airplay, as of September 26, 1977. It was the first time that my name and on-air persona..."Stef in the Night Time"...was printed on the survey.

77

Reporter for WLNY-TV / New York, Fall 1996.

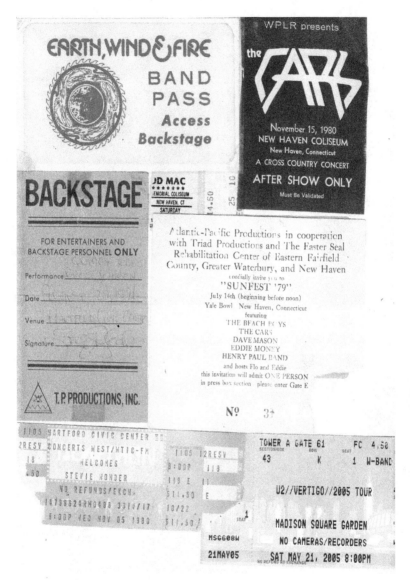

Some of the great perks of working in radio: concert tickets, backstage passes, and meeting many famous people.

My wife Victoria, Billy Joel, and me,
backstage at the New Haven Coliseum, 1984.

My wife Victoria, Barry Manilow, and me,
backstage at the Hartford Civic Center, 1985.

June 1984: my wife Victoria and me, backstage at the Hartford Civic Center with Tina Turner; she was the opening act for Lionel Richie on this tour.

My wife Victoria and me with Kenny Rogers, backstage at the Coliseum in New Haven, Connecticut, Fall 1983.

My wife Victoria, Lionel Richie, and me, backstage at the Hartford Civic Center, June 1986.

February 1987: Backstage at the Hartford Civic Center with Phil Collins, who was performing in concert with Genesis.

With Michael Bolton at the nightclub Toad's Place in New Haven, Connecticut, celebrating the release of his Soul Provider *album, Summer 1989.*

Singer Amy Grant and me, Summer 1994, in New York City, celebrating the release of her album House of Love.

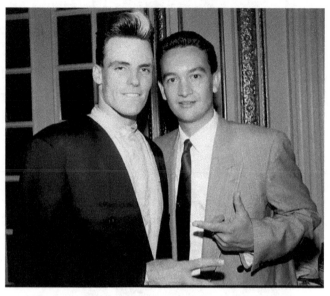

*Vanilla Ice and me, September 1990, at the National
Association of Broadcasters Convention in Boston. His song
"Ice Ice Baby" had just been released and would quickly take
him to the top of the music charts and instant fame.*

*With Mariah Carey in Los Angeles, late Spring/early
Summer 1990, celebrating the release of her first
single,* Vision of Love. *She was 19 years old at the
time and dreaming of making it big someday.*

My wife Victoria, Donny Osmond, and me at a private party in Hamden, Connecticut, in the Spring of 1989, celebrating the release of his self-titled comeback album, which yielded the hit songs Soldier of Love *and* Sacred Emotion.

Eddie Money and me, backstage at an outdoor concert that he performed on Long Island in the Summer of 2011.

Peter Noone, who became famous as the lead singer of the 1960's group Herman's Hermits, backstage at an outdoor concert he performed on Long Island in the Summer of 2011.

With John Oates at radio station KC101, New Haven, Connecticut, 1982.

With Daryl Hall, Spring 1991, Phoenix, Arizona.

*November 8, 1994: with award-winning songwriter Martin Page.
This is the first time we met, and we hit it off instantly, talking
about all of the great songs that Martin's written and legendary
performers he's worked with.*

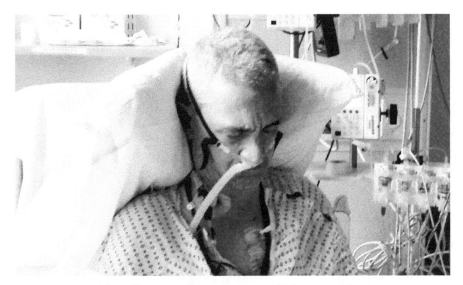

Me, after open heart surgery, February 2016,
at the Weill Cornell Medical Center, NYC.

Brother Larry Lussier, CSC: my teacher,
mentor, spiritual counselor, and dear friend.

CHAPTER
TWELVE

As you may have gathered by now, this is a book about surviving unexpected difficulties—difficulties that are utterly impossible to predict ahead of time. I've come up with a name for these difficulties. I call them "war zones."

People can become war zones for each other, often without even trying. I want to go into a little more depth about the large war zone that my father came to define for my family and me.

My father was a military man at heart, a man whom one crossed at one's own peril. That is not the same thing as being an evil man. It can, however, make family life difficult. My father was deeply scarred due to living through his war zones, though I don't have anywhere near the level of detail of those war zones that I do about my mother's and my own. That uncertainty now parallels a similar, more anxious uncertainty from when I was growing up.

I loved my father, but I found myself terrified of what he might be about to do for much of my life. He could make life miserable for family members who ignored his authority or disobeyed his commands. And that is the right word. My father didn't make suggestions or pass along instructions to us. He commanded, and he expected to be obeyed, immediately and without question or hesitation.

Let me clarify. My father was not a monster, but what he witnessed during World War II was man's monstrous inhumanity to man, and it affected him deeply for the rest of his life. As I grew up, I had plenty of moments living in fear of his rage. My dad was a frozen lake ready to snap, collapse, and take me under. One walked across such a surface with great trepidation and great care.

And yet there were moments when his love was clear to me. They tended to be silent moments. He was a man who often seemed lost in deep thought. Yes, he could be talkative, but those talks would usually turn into intense debates, even over the silliest things, with my father believing that his viewpoint was and would always be unquestionably correct. Not wanting to debate him and never wanting to be subjected to one of his stern lectures, I learned how to hold my tongue. As a result, my father and I never really engaged in very much small talk. That sounds awful, but it is the truth of the matter. That said, I do recall several occasions as a young boy when he took me fishing, and the two of us were able to enjoy the deep silence and the profound peace of the outdoors as the extraordinary gifts they are. I always felt accepted and cared for, and I felt deep joy in being alone with him. The long silences meant that I couldn't say the wrong thing and cause an explosion. It was as though he was going out of his way to find an environment in which we could say nothing to each other and be happy finding a connection in that.

There were times where his friends would come over, gather around a table, and play cards. As a young boy, I was entranced by their easy camaraderie, their mastery of the intricate ritual of the game, their stories about growing up in Poland and living through the war, and most of all their ability to tease each other without setting any major argument off. My father seemed to enjoy allowing me to be an observer at these sessions. Again, I came to love and look forward to these evenings because I didn't have to say anything and thus could count on not saying anything that would set him off.

I can recall my father on Christmas Eve, behind a closed door, "talking" to Santa Claus in the hallway, who was "interviewing" him about whether or not we children had behaved. In later years, of course, I learned that my father had played both himself and Santa. I remember the years when I knew the secret with much fondness because I knew my father was doing something nice for us. Again, I didn't have to say anything. He always said nice things about us to Santa, though he did drop the occasional hint about how we could improve. What parent wouldn't?

These were childhood memories, however. A child will go out of his way to find opportunities to look up to his father, and he and my mother made sure I got those opportunities. They reminded me of how proud I should be of their having survived World War II and of how proud I should be of being Polish. If I knew there were things in our lives that I wasn't so proud of, and I suppose I did, I kept those to myself.

When your parents are locked in a relationship that they each increasingly loathe, you have suspicions as a child, but you learn to tune them out. As an adult, you come to find that tuning-out process more difficult. Once I was talking to my sister Barbara about our father. I don't remember the exact year. I know I was in my early twenties, and she was in her early thirties. We talked about why our parents had divorced, a topic that my mother had danced around whenever I brought it up with her one-on-one. No matter what age I reached, she always considered me the baby of the family and shielded me from information that she thought would be painful or hurtful for me to know. However, Barbara could be counted on to tell me the truth, the whole truth, and nothing but the truth once I'd crossed the threshold into adulthood. So, it was then that I finally learned, as a young adult, that Barbara had heard through her bedroom wall, when my father believed her to be asleep, what we today would call a sexual assault upon my mother. Put simply, my mother did not want to have sex, my father did, and as Barbara listened (without wanting to), he won the argument, over deep objections.

I was glad I hadn't heard that scene and glad, too, that my mother had declined to mention it to me when she had the chance. Both Barbara and I suspected that the incident was not the only one of its kind.

Knowing what had happened, what his various war zones had led him to, brought me into a new realm of sadness concerning my father. I never hated him, not even after learning from Barbara about that awful night. I did feel angry, though, at the many choices he made that deeply hurt my mother. I never talked to him about the event I'd learned from Barbara, but my father and I started to keep each other at arm's length.

On my wedding day, as my wife and I were dancing for the first time as a married couple, I noticed my father putting on his jacket and getting ready to leave the reception—ridiculously early. I ran over to him and asked, "Tata, what's the matter? Where are you going?" (*Tata* is the Polish word for Dad.)

His eyes flashed—I knew that aggrieved anger well—and he said, "I have to leave. I don't want to talk about it," as he pursed his lips tight.

"Come on, Tata. It's my wedding day. You seem upset. Please tell me what's going on."

But he didn't. No matter what I did, I couldn't get an explanation, and I couldn't get a different decision. He stalked away. Years later, I learned that he had been personally offended because my wife and I had not visited the table where he was sitting at the reception as quickly as he thought we should have. Unknowingly, we didn't follow the protocol that my father had set in his mind, so he felt deeply offended, and he showed it by storming out of the wedding reception. That's the way it was with him. One had no idea what would send you hurtling into the next major piece of drama with him. In recent years, it's occurred to me that he probably imagined he was doing me a great favor by not answering my questions, not telling me what was wrong. He probably thought that he would make the day worse by speaking out, which of course, he would have. He probably expected me to be grateful for him simply leaving without shouting at me on my wedding day.

Some people get close to others with well-chosen words. For my father, though, words were, all too often, the trip wires that set off explosions or the lines that defined the borders of the nearest war zone. In his much later years, he did his best to disengage from communicating altogether to avoid those zones, and he often seemed so distant, so lost in his thoughts.

The older I get, the easier it is for me to accept my father's two most relevant truths. He was a fundamentally decent man, and at the same time, he was inherently abusive.

When you're a young person, two possibilities like that seem contradictory and mutually exclusive, especially about someone in your family. You can't imagine both of them being realities at the same time. You assume that somehow one of them will cancel out the other. With the benefit of time, though, you realize that people are complicated and opposing traits exist within all of us, and for some people, the contradiction is just part of the essence of who they are. I now know that's how it was in my father's case. He was extreme in both his decency and in his abuse. I can't imagine what it must have been like for my mother to have to come to terms with this seemingly impossible state of affairs, given that I am only beginning to come to terms with it myself. I have a lot of respect for my mother finding her way through those two difficult truths—a high regard I would not have been capable of holding when I was younger.

When I was about 10 or 11 years old, my father made a point of sharing his advice with me about dealing with women. When it came to social niceties and the fairer sex, he was what we now call "old school." He made a point of giving me little mini-lessons about the right and the wrong way to treat female acquaintances, and he frequently talked about how important it was that I understand and embrace these practices. He would tell me things like, "If you meet a woman and she holds out her hand, you should take her hand in your own, bow slightly, and kiss her hand with great tenderness. Then you should let go of the hand and stand up straight and tall, like a knight in armor. Women love that kind of thing. They love when you show them that kind of respect. They see you as a true gentleman."

That's the kind of thing he taught me, and it was all strangely out of place. I never ran into one woman who extended her hand, waiting for it to be kissed. Not one. I filed such lessons under the heading, "How My Father Lived His Life." There were a lot of entries in that file, and I imagined that none of them had any meaningful lessons for me.

As the years have passed, I have come to understand that there actually was an important lesson from my father in all those little lectures I got. It wasn't the kind of lesson he imagined he was sharing with me, though.

There's a bitter, inescapable irony built into his advice about men maintaining excruciating politeness and respect in their dealings with the opposite sex: It was all an act. Beyond the formal courtesies that he was so good at and so insistent upon, he didn't actually show the women in his life much, or any, respect. And I knew I didn't want to live my life like that.

All of the "respect" he showed women, and specifically to my mother, lay on the surface. In reality, he showed women little or no respect. He was an epic philanderer, and he was sexually abusive toward my mother. I know that now. And writing this book has helped me to come to terms with it.

This was their life. This was what my mother experienced living with him. It must have been a painful and bitter trial for her even to attempt to make that marriage work for as long as she did.

My father was good at keeping up a façade. One of my strongest memories is of him insisting, with my mother, that we all dress up in our Sunday best and go to church. Yet my father always waited outside for us. He didn't set foot in the church on these days. He sat in the car, reading the newspaper, chain-smoking cigarettes.

CHAPTER THIRTEEN

I've shared with you my belief that my father was a fundamentally decent man. Even though his formal etiquette posturing and his empty Catholicism were part of an elaborate act, I do believe that, at the core of his being, my father was someone who tried to do the right thing and sometimes managed to accomplish that.

There was one particular occasion when I was in my early twenties that my father and I were all alone. I was visiting him in Michigan, where he lived. My father was driving; he pulled the car over for no apparent reason, set the brake, and stared straight ahead for a long moment. There was a peculiar, unanticipated, and striking intimacy in the silence, as though we were fishing again. But this time, he had something to say.

He turned his head, looked me in the eye, and said, "Stefan, I never loved your mother. We met right after the war; we had both been through a lot; we were two healthy young adults. I was attracted to her. We slept together. Your mother got pregnant, and I had a decision to make. I chose to do the right thing. That was the way it was. But I never loved her."

I recall that as a strange and one-sided conversation. I had no coherent reply. How could I have? I honestly don't remember what I said in response to those words from my father. I suspect that I just nodded and changed the subject. I was at the age when I was figuring out sexuality and relationships for myself, which I suppose is why my father shared that confession with me.

I'm sure there were plenty of people who, having impregnated a young and beautiful woman in the months immediately following World War II, ran away from responsibility. My father wasn't one of them. He had tried to do the right thing by my mother. He thought he was doing the right thing by me in telling me about his decision. Maybe he was. I believe my father tried to be a good person, even though he knew there were times when he wasn't sure he would pull it off.

It would have been considerably easier for me, and for my mother, I suppose, if he had been all one thing or all the other. But that's not the way it worked out. People are shades of gray. I do know now, with a certainty I never had before I started working on this book, that one of my mother's main goals in life was to raise me as a man who would treat women with real respect, not the illusion of it. I hope she succeeded. On my better days, I believe she did.

One of the things I will never know is the degree to which my father's elaborate, external politeness toward women he was meeting for the first time was something that my mother experienced during their initial interaction. I think it must have been. I picture him kissing her hand and bowing with formal grace during their very first meeting after she got off that bicycle and walked over to the place where he was standing and watching her. I then imagine him releasing her hand and standing there like the knight in shining armor she must have believed him to be.

I am chronicling the aspects of my mother's life that didn't make a hell of a lot of sense, and my father heads the list. He was the one significant, senseless phenomenon that my mother and I shared intimately.

My father was a strict military man with a wounded mind. He took the concept of discipline to an obsessive, unhealthy, and irrational level in our home. My memory is that there was virtually nothing I did growing up that my father didn't critique, debate, and criticize. Even if it was a good thing I'd done, I knew he would find some way to tear it apart. Whatever I came up with, my father would find something about it that proved I had come up short. "What in the world did you think when you decided to get your hair cut that way? Don't you realize how silly you look? What's the matter with you?"

My mother offered her share of criticism, too, but my father was the dictatorial grandmaster. From a very young age, I felt like I was on the defensive whenever I was in his company. It didn't get any better as I grew into adulthood. It wasn't a very pleasant way to go through life.

I think the deep, painful, seemingly perpetual criticism existed in our household because both of my parents were imperfect survivors of what would today be called severe traumatic stress. Each of them had different ways of dealing with and processing that trauma. Each of them sometimes couldn't help sharing critical comments with people they loved in a way that didn't sound like love. My father's mode of expression was particularly brutal and obsessive. My father criticized my mother for everything. One night she happened to serve rice for dinner, and he suddenly became furious about the insensitivity and cruelty of her culinary choices. Didn't she know he hated rice? (No one had known before that moment.) What on earth did she have against him? As far as any of us could tell, she had only been trying to make him, and us, happy by making a nice dinner. What kind of wife was she, to go out of her way to serve her husband something horrible like rice?

Everything my mother did seemed to develop into a significant issue with my father. In his mind, there was always some terrible crime she'd committed. She simply couldn't catch a break from the man.

He stomped away from the table.

Once, when I was about nine or 10 years old, I had come home from school for lunch. This was back in the day when schools would let kids go home for lunch. My father would pick us up and bring us home, and my mother would have something nice waiting for us on the table. It was a warm and welcome ritual. On this occasion, though, I remember finishing my lunch and noticing my father looking at my shoes with a deepening, angry scowl.

I thought to myself, *Uh-oh.*

The school had somewhat of a dress code, and I was wearing black leather shoes. Since my father was a military guy, he expected shoes that were highly polished. It turned out that my shoes were not polished to his complete satisfaction. They weren't spit-shined. Several smudges were visible from several feet away.

He started in on me. *Did I realize my shoes were not correctly polished? What the hell was I thinking, going to school with shoes that weren't adequately polished? What did I want people to say about our family? That we were a bunch of slobs? Hadn't he shown me how to polish my shoes properly? Did I think I could get away with acting like a slob?*

My father had risen out of his chair. He was towering over me, enraged and shouting. I kept thinking. *Maybe he won't hit me. Maybe he won't hit me. Maybe he won't...*

But he did. He started slapping me around the room with such force that I began to cry. I cried so hard I could barely breathe. I don't remember a lot that happened the rest of that day.

That's the way it was with my father. You never knew what was going to happen. You were always moving from side to side trying to avoid the next irrational assault. It always came. You just didn't know when. I grew up in fear of my father.

Up to this point, I had looked at all of this from a child's perspective. I had never put two and two together. I never realized that my mother must have lived in the same state of constant alarm and paranoia that I did. She must have been in constant fear for herself and her children. Her longest, least escapable war zone was what she faced whenever my father was in the house. How could it not have been?

That volcanic, impossible-to-predict temper was, of course, just another item in the long list of war zone impossibilities in my mother's life. Some people see a list like that and conclude that life must be pretty much meaningless, a series of random events. But that's not the way my mother saw her life, and it's not how I see my life, either.

CHAPTER
FOURTEEN

In the years after my father left us, during the time I was in high school and college, I realized my mother had two primary ways of handling stress. These two strategies allowed her to cope with the intense financial and emotional pressures that she encountered as an overworked, hourly-wage-earning, underpaid single mom who also happened to be a survivor of major trauma and abuse. My mother used dancing and alcohol to deal with stress. I preferred it when she was dancing.

We had a Sunday morning ritual that I particularly loved because it inevitably led to my mother, my sister Jane, and me dancing together in the kitchen. My mother would insist on taking Jane and me to the 8:00 a.m. Mass at St. Stanislaus, which was the local Polish church. That Mass was conducted in Polish, and my mother felt it was one way to keep in touch with our Polish heritage. It didn't matter how late we stayed up on Saturday night; my mother got us up at 7:00 a.m. sharp each Sunday, and she made sure that we were washed, dressed, and ready to go. Heaven forbid that we were tired and moving slowly before going to Mass!

My mother insisted that we get to the church early so that we could sit in the very front pew on the right-hand side of the church, close to the altar. As far as my mother was concerned, that was *our* seat, and she made sure we got to St. Stan's well before Mass started so that no one else would sit there.

One of these Sunday mornings, I recall my mother being quite restless. Looking back, I don't know if this was because of the pressures of the unpaid bills that could have been pressing in on her mind, or if she was hungover from drinking the night before, or if it was a combination of the two. Suffice it to say, my mother was out of sorts at this particular Mass.

Father Luke was a visiting priest from Poland who had become a bit of a family friend; he would come to the house for dinner every now and then. As Father Luke droned on and on during his sermon, my mother became even more agitated. Finally, my mother said, out loud, in Polish, right there from the front pew, in front of everyone else who was in attendance, "Luke! You're repeating yourself! Finish your sermon and finish Mass!" With that, Father Luke paused briefly, abruptly ended his sermon, and rushed through the rest of the Mass as quickly as he possibly could. I don't recall him ever coming to our house again for dinner.

After every Mass, we'd drive a few blocks from the church, and go to Stanley's Bakery and get a big order of cake, pastries, bread, and rolls. Then we would come home and go into the kitchen, and my mother would make us brunch, using the food that we just bought at the bakery. My God, did it taste good!

While we were eating brunch, my mother would put on the Polish music show on WATR, a local radio station that played Polish music for two solid hours on Sunday mornings. Looking back, I suspect that Polish radio show was one of the reasons why it was so important that we attend the early Mass—so we could all have plenty of time to listen to the Polish music once we made it back home. Very often, my mother's favorite polka songs would come on, and the three of us—my mother, my sister Jane, and me—would dance together in the kitchen. This was a Sunday morning tradition that was special to us. When the Polish radio show was over, so was brunch, and we went on with our day.

That wasn't the only dancing my mother did, though. On many Sunday evenings, she and her friends would go out to a local Polish hall and dance to a live Polka band. Then, every summer, the three of us went to the Polish Picnic, where many people from around the state, many of whom were of Polish descent, gathered at the Polish Community Park for the annual festival.

For reasons I can't quite recall, there was a moment at this festival when the dance floor was completely empty while the Polka band played. My mother, wanting to enliven the festivities, told my sister Jane, "Watch this!" She tapped me on the shoulder, took my hand, and led me out onto the dance floor, where she proceeded to astonish the assembled gathering with her vintage dance moves, which I had to assume she had mastered back in the day, with my father.

I was her partner on that dance floor. I knew I couldn't execute or even anticipate the kinds of fancy moves that she was pulling off. I doubted that anyone could, but I had been dancing with her long enough in the kitchen to know roughly where she needed me to be and when she needed me to be there. Every eye in the room was following us. No matter where we went, I was always in the right place, and she seemed to be facing toward heaven, whichever way she turned.

I heard someone in the audience say, in a loud and approving voice with a Polish accent, "Bravo! Beautiful dancing!" The song ended, and the room erupted in applause as we made it back to our table. I think we might have been floating rather than walking. A woman seated next to us leaned over, grinned broadly, and said to my mother, "That was so very nice. Do you get paid to dance here?" Without missing a beat, my mother smiled broadly and said, "Not yet!" Then she laughed loudly enough and long enough for Jane and me to start laughing too. If you'd been there and asked me what we were all laughing at, I couldn't have told you. Now I realize that we were laughing at the world beyond that dance floor. We were laughing at the world of unpaid bills, absent fathers, and long hours of work with low pay and unpredictable disaster. It was a world that seemed small and powerless and far away from the three of us at that moment.

I suppose there's a lot that I could be writing here about my mother's second stress management technique, alcohol, but it seems unfair for me to spend any more time than necessary on her drinking. It's enough for me to use this chapter to confirm what I bet you could have easily figured out for yourself, that my mother could say some cruel and hurtful things when she drank. She drank a lot, and often drank alone. When my mother drank, she always made me wish that she were dancing instead.

CHAPTER
FIFTEEN

All things considered, my mother was a very positive person, which was remarkable given everything that she had suffered through in her life. One of the critical habits for coping, and yes, for survival, that she instilled in me was her ability to look on the bright side of just about any problem and see a challenge as something that had presented itself for a reason. As human beings, she believed that our job was to assume that the reason would eventually become clear to us. We should be open to the possibilities and the lessons that other people might not see, and we should try to find a reason to laugh or smile along the way.

When my father left us, my mother's own ability to look on the bright side sometimes collapsed. She went through a period where she sometimes had very tough days because of the heavy financial pressures.

My father lived in another state, and he wasn't paying child support. He wasn't taking responsibility for his family. My mother had to watch out for all of us, which couldn't have been easy. She had to make the mortgage payments and put food on the table. She worked long hours as a cook in a local restaurant, and she didn't earn a lot. Sometimes this depressed her, and sometimes when I caught her in an unguarded moment, it looked like she wanted to give up. It was a certain way she held her face, and it made me feel awful.

Looking back, I can't really blame her for being depressed. She was a single mother working full-time. The job she had was an hourly position. That meant she didn't get paid if she missed work. This put her under enormous pressure. I remember one winter morning when there were at least six inches of snow on the ground, perhaps more. The school I attended was canceled. The restaurant where my mother worked was in a mall. The streets weren't plowed. My mother couldn't drive to work. She left me at home to keep an eye on Jane, and she trudged off to work, on foot, through the snow. That night, she trudged back. It had been at least a challenging, three-mile walk each way through the chilly winter streets.

The next morning, when I came downstairs, I saw that my mother was utterly exhausted. I think she might have been up all night worrying about some bill she had to pay. She was sitting at the kitchen table listening to one of her favorite radio stations, a station that played dance music from the forties and fifties. She had that look on her face that said she felt like giving up. The expression was only there for a second. When she saw me, it vanished.

I knew she was distraught and deeply tired of worrying and that she needed an emotional lift. She looked more like an old woman.

I walked over to the radio, turned it up, grabbed her by the arm, and said, "Come on, Mama. Let's dance."

She didn't resist. She stood up as though she had somehow been transformed into a teenager. She loved dancing.

In one moment, my mother's face was beaming again. We were happy, and we were safe, and we were dancing to Glenn Miller's "In the Mood," and the kitchen was our dance floor. As we circled, spun, laughed, and effortlessly moved our feet to the rhythm of that marvelous song, I could tell that all my mother's cares and pressures of the day had vanished. She didn't have to worry about my father not loving her anymore, or the bills she had to pay, or whether it was going to snow again, or how many hours she had on the schedule at the restaurant. We were happy, and somehow, we were going to be all right.

From the way my mother laughed, I could tell that I had made her day. I promised myself to notice when the cares and concerns of the day seemed to be getting the better of her. I made a commitment to check in on her in the morning and to dance with her whenever it looked like she was giving up. I did my best to keep that promise. That day marked the beginning of our dancing mornings. Whenever I'd notice that she was feeling low, I would ask her to dance.

She always accepted.

After a couple of weeks, I worked up my courage and changed the radio from her oldies station to WWCO, the Top 40 Station I liked listening to. She protested at first, but I insisted.

"Mama, we don't have to dance to Glenn Miller all the time," I said, twiddling the knob on the radio.

Her eyes seemed to say, *Okay, if you say so.* She was skeptical, but I could tell she still wanted to dance, and she wanted to make me happy.

I found WWCO, and immediately recognized the song that was just starting to play.

"Perfect!" I said. "We can dance to this. I love this song."

My mother made a bit of a disapproving grimace on her face and said she couldn't possibly dance to the song. Eventually, she gave in, smiled and followed my lead. Now we were dancing to my kind of music, even though my mother remained dubious about rock and roll.

After about thirty seconds, my mother asked, "What the heck do you call this song?"

"Mama, it's called "The Joker." It's by Steve Miller."

"Steve Miller? Is he Glenn Miller's son?"

"No, Mama, I don't think so."

"Well, if he is, I can tell you this much. He didn't learn to write music from his father because *this* is not music!" I laughed and shrugged my shoulders. To each his own.

We both kept right on dancing until "The Joker" got to the bridge of the song, at which point my mother stopped dancing and began laughing hysterically.

"What are you laughing about?" I asked.

"Who writes *words* like that?"

"What? What's wrong with the words, Mama?"

"'Lovey-dovey, lovey-dovey, lovey-dovey, all the time,' did he get *paid* for writing that?"

Yes, Mama. He got paid a lot of money. Come on. Let's keep dancing."

She did, but she couldn't stop laughing as she moved. As we danced, she made me promise that at the end of the song I'd change the radio from WWCO back to her oldies station.

"I don't know how you can listen to that station," she said. "'Lovey-dovey, lovey-dovey.' What crazy words! Who dances to that?" But she was grinning as she said that. "You and this WWCO. You're made for each other." She was right. We were made for each other, but I didn't realize it yet.

My mother looked beautiful as she danced. She also looked young and happy. She was getting the hang of the dancing part and the making-each-other-happy-when-it-was-time-to-do-that part. She was looking on the bright side again. Life was good, and all seemed well during these precious moments.

CHAPTER
SIXTEEN

For Thanksgiving of 1980 to make sense to you, you need to understand how I swerved hard into what the Eagles band immortalized in their song "Life in the Fast Lane." And to understand that, you have to know the innocence of how I got into radio.

It was 1975, my junior year at Holy Cross High School in Waterbury, Connecticut. I was looking for an elective course to take, preferably one where I wouldn't have to work too hard. You see, even though I played on the school basketball team in my freshman year and got cut in my sophomore year, I still had somewhat of a "jock mentality" going into my junior year. That mindset caused me to choose an elective where, hopefully, I wouldn't have to work too hard but still get a good grade.

As I went down the list of available electives, I saw a course called Mass Media 101. The description said it was a general overview of radio, television, and print. I thought, *Hey, that sounds good. I like listening to the radio and watching TV. I like* Rolling Stone *magazine. This is going to be a fun course, and the homework will probably be minimal and easy. I'll sign up for that.* So, I did.

Little did I know.

I neglected to find out who was teaching the course. When I walked into class, I spotted the man I least wanted to see at the front of the room. It was Brother Larry Lussier.

Previously, I'd taken an English course with Brother Larry, and the instant he came into the very first class, I knew exactly what he was going to be like: strict, demanding, challenging, with everything done by the book. To use a word that was used a lot back in those days, Brother Larry was a *hardass*. A complete and total hardass. He was disciplined, organized, and efficient. He expected that same level of attention to detail from his students. He was not the guy you wanted to teach a course that you thought would be fun and easy, with little or no homework.

The bell rang. At the front of the room, Brother Larry stood firmly and studied us. He waited for the room to fall silent. When it had, he asked in his calm, but somewhat stern voice,

"So, gentlemen, are you ready for Mass Media 101?"

We all nodded yes, but not quite sure of our answer, based on who was teaching the course. Brother Larry seemed to catch my eye. Then he said, "Very good, but rest assured, I'm going to keep my eye on you the entire semester."

And the lesson began in earnest. Brother Larry hadn't been going for more than thirty seconds before I wrote this sentence in my notebook, "I just can't catch a break here." I also made a mental note to drop the class and pick another elective.

But for some reason, after the first class wrapped up, I *didn't* drop it. To this day, I couldn't give you an apparent reason why. I guess my closest explanation was that there was something deep inside me that told me I was supposed to stay in that class—even though I'd made up my mind that I'd already had more than enough of Brother Larry Hardass.

As I expected, he really made me work. But he had a way of making us work on things that mattered to us, so the hardass problem became less of an issue.

Here is a case in point. Brother Larry had found out how much I loved radio and found out what my favorite station was. Eventually, he gave me a semester project designed specifically for me. I was to spend a significant amount of time with a disc jockey at a local station of my choice. I was to watch him do his job for a couple of days and accompany him on remote broadcasts to see what and how he did things. I needed to see how he interacted with listeners on the phone and at station events in the community. I was also supposed to take pictures. I was to get a real sense, first-hand experience of what a disk jockey's life was like. Then I needed to write it all up like a newspaper article, edit it carefully, and turn it in.

It all seemed like a lot of work, and I told him so.

"That's because it *is* a lot of work. You're going to do it, though, Stefan, because I believe *you* are the perfect man for this project."

That, apparently, settled that.

Resigned to my fate, I chose WWCO, a local radio station that played my favorite music: the Top 40 hits. I figured that if I was going to do all of the work that Brother Larry insisted, I might as well spend my time learning about a station I actually listened to. The disk jockey I called was named Tom Collins. On the phone, I told him what Brother Larry wanted me to do. Tom readily agreed to let me spend the time with him.

That project Brother Larry pushed me to complete, changed my life. It took me entirely by surprise. It stopped feeling like work and quickly became a labor of love and excitement. Up until my junior year at Holy Cross, playing sports was very important to me. But the more I learned about radio, the more it seemed that it might just be my calling in life. There came the point where I said to myself, *You know, I'm never going to be one of the world's greatest athletes, but I'd love to get involved with this radio thing; I'd like to become a disc jockey like Tom Collins. He's only about four years older than me, anyway.*

I fell hard for radio. The whole world that Tom Collins and the other disc jockeys at WWCO lived in just captivated me. By the end of that semester project, I realized that being in radio was the best possible way for me to make a living and have a whole bunch of fun!

Tom Collins and Danny Lyons, two popular 'CO disc jockeys, became very good friends of mine. They took me in under their wings and showed me the ropes. When my junior year ended, I was hanging out at the radio station as much as possible. I guess you could say that I was an intern, but I was really a glorified gopher. I didn't care because it allowed me to spend a lot of time at the station.

Two years later, when I was in my freshman year in college at the University of Bridgeport as a journalism communication major, an opening came up at WWCO for an overnight disc jockey. I got the job!

I had Brother Larry to thank for it, and I told him so one day, after the last class of the semester. He could have assigned anyone that WWCO radio project, but he chose me because he took the time to learn what truly interested me. I told him I knew that not every teacher did that, and that even though I'd been skeptical about the class at first because I didn't feel like doing a lot of work, I was glad that he had pushed me the way he did.

Brother Larry, who was gathering papers from his desk, paused to look at me, smiled, and said, "I'm not done pushing you, Stefan."

I said, "What do you mean, Brother?"

He said, "I mean that you're on your way now, kid. We just need to make sure that you keep heading in the right direction. Please keep me updated on your activities, okay?"

I nodded instantly, and said, "Absolutely, Brother. I'll keep in touch."

But there was something in Brother Larry's expression that said, *I know you think you mean that, but I'm going to keep my eye on you anyway.*

CHAPTER
SEVENTEEN

There came a time when I decided to tune out my own better judgment. Let me set the stage for how this happened. Like many people coming of age in the 1970s, I was seeing all of the changes that were happening in modern society, specifically, the changes in attitudes about sex and drugs, and what it meant for me personally. I had a severely dysfunctional relationship with my father, who was almost entirely absent from my life, and I also had a complicated relationship with my mother. Her status as an increasingly hardcore alcoholic was getting harder for me to ignore. Add it all up, and the result was a perfect landscape for a pretty big series of shifts that happened in my life, not all of them entirely well thought out, and not all of them altogether healthy.

Suffice it to say that when an opportunity presented itself for me to forge an entirely new identity rooted in radio, the medium I had grown to love due to that high school project that Brother Larry assigned to me, I went for it. I became "Stef in the Night Time," the young, cool, hip, slick, sexy, smooth-talking radio personality on WWCO radio.

Eventually, I started hiding things. A little voice inside me kept telling me that what I was doing was wrong, but I always found ways not to listen to that little voice.

I told myself I had a right not to listen. I had been listening to that voice all my life. I was a clean-cut, 19-year-old kid. I was the product of the Catholic education system, a former altar boy, someone who had worn uniforms to school for as long as he could remember. Maybe it was time for a change.

Hadn't I worked hard and put up with a lot? Of course, I had. Hadn't the general manager of the radio station told me he liked my attitude and work ethic? Hadn't he told me he liked my style and that "all the ladies in town" loved the sound of my voice? He thought that I could go far in the radio industry if I wanted to, and he asked me whether I really wanted to be in radio, and do all the things that popular DJs do? It turned out those questions weren't all that hard for me to answer. So, my life changed.

Suddenly I was in charge of the late-night shift at the hottest music radio station in Waterbury, Connecticut. I was playing all of the hits and living my dream. And you know what? If I wasn't entirely happy, well, at least I was distracted.

So what if my dad still was out of the picture and my sister Jane wasn't doing as well as she could have been? So what if my mother was drinking more than ever and I sometimes felt like I just couldn't handle any of that? I didn't have to. I was loving what I was doing. I was 'Stef in the Night Time.'

I had a feeling for some time that my mother's drinking was getting worse and that I needed to do something about that, but I had decided that I didn't really have to focus on that if I didn't want to. So I tuned that voice out. Instead, I focused on what I liked. It was my night shift work at WWCO. I was a star, or so I thought, in my own hometown.

Truth be told, now that I had become a disc jockey, I was an increasingly absent feature in our household. One afternoon I came home from running some errands to find my sister Jane sitting hunched over in front of the television, crying her eyes out. She was sobbing uncontrollably, and I didn't know why.

The television show Jane was watching was *The Newlywed Game,* and I had to admit that a program like that didn't seem all that likely to produce that kind of intense emotional response from Jane. Something was wrong. So instead of going straight to my room and closing the door, which is what I usually did when I came home these days, I asked, "What's the matter, Jane?"

She said, "Mama is sick."

Pretty tough to ignore that one.

I said, "Where?"

She said, "Upstairs."

I went upstairs to check on our mother, and I discovered she wasn't sick. She was drunk, and she could barely speak. She was drunker than I could ever remember seeing her before, which was seriously damn drunk.

I tried to get my mother focused and told her that it was time for me to go back downstairs and get her some ginger ale, but I wasn't making a lot of headway. I took a deep breath and felt my stomach twist into several knots. *Why in the world did I have to deal with this? Why couldn't she take care of herself for a change? How long would this downward cycle go on?*

Then the front doorbell rang. I made my way downstairs. It was Roland, a long-time friend of the family. He just happened to be driving through our neighborhood and decided to stop by for a quick visit. He wanted to know if my mother was home.

I explained to Roland that my mother wasn't feeling so well. I was too embarrassed to tell him that she was utterly sloshed. Something in my demeanor must have tipped Roland off that we had a bigger problem than I was letting on because he shook his head like he didn't quite buy my explanation. He announced that he was going upstairs to check on my mother. Roland said he had a feeling that something was wrong in our house and he wouldn't be able to forgive himself if he left without seeing his friend Maria.

My stomach churned again. I tried to stop Roland from going upstairs, but I couldn't bring myself to block his way. I followed him up and into the room that my mother was lying in.

The minute Roland saw my mother, he said, "Maria, what's the matter?"

Without missing a beat, my mother said, "Roland, I'm drunk."

It wasn't funny. It was completely humiliating. Now someone else outside the immediate family would know. My stomach knotted up even more, and I could feel myself turning red-faced in total embarrassment.

That little voice inside me said, *This isn't about you. It's about Mama. Jane was right after all. Mama is sick, and she needs help.*

At that moment, though, I really didn't want to hear another word from that little voice. I went back downstairs, left Roland to deal with my mother, walked out of the house, got in my car, and hit the road. I needed the drive to clear my head.

From that day forward, I looked for ways not having to deal with my mother, and I was pretty good at finding them. I also stopped returning Brother Larry's calls that came in like clockwork, once every couple of weeks. I just didn't want to deal with any of it. I kept telling myself I needed to clear my head.

I was learning the ropes in the world of radio at WWCO. My show was getting popular, and I received a better time slot. The general manager was happy with my performance. I was going to concerts and meeting famous singers because I had backstage passes. I was meeting groupies, smoking pot, snorting cocaine, and taking speed pills. The excuse that I gave myself for my new lifestyle was that all of this was acceptable behavior for a "hot rockin', flame throwin'" Top 40 disc jockey. Sex, drugs, and rock and roll were the norm; at least that's what I convinced myself of.

A little voice inside of me kept pointing out that, despite my best efforts from the day I followed Roland up to my mother's room and in all the days that came after, my head wasn't getting any clearer. On the contrary, it was getting murkier, foggier, and more confused with every passing day, and the guy who kept looking back at me in the mirror was becoming more difficult for me to recognize. However, I tuned that voice out.

I didn't realize it at the time, but I know now that the strange new identity I was forging for myself, "Stef in the Night Time," was my own response to all the stresses I had experienced growing up—not just my mother's descent into deep alcoholism. Those traumas I went through were unique to me, of course, and maybe they were nothing compared to what others had gone through, but they were something I had to work out. The traumas were painful and pervasive enough for me to begin a pattern of self-medication that led me to start hiding significant parts of my life from the two people who meant the world to me— my mother and Brother Larry.

The voice inside said, *Something's gotta give.*

But I kept tuning it out.

Which brings us to Thanksgiving of 1980.

CHAPTER
EIGHTEEN

The late seventies were kind of a blur to me.

On the outside, it appeared that I was developing into a mature, responsible young man. However, inside was a slow-spreading fog that would, at times, recede long enough for me to perform specific roles. I was the son who checked in and occasionally danced with his mother, the brother who made sure his developmentally-disabled sister was okay, the relative who showed up at important family events and cracked jokes, and the disc jockey who stood behind a microphone and hosted a radio program in Waterbury, Connecticut. But when the show was over, I got sucked back into that blur. Eventually, I materialized only for my on-air shift, radio station events, nightclub appearances, and deejaying dances and parties. Everything else was a kind of a sustained, chemically-induced fadeout.

I must admit that much of what happened to me during this period I've forgotten. I'm not sure if that's a good or a bad thing. I suspect there are things I'd rather not recall. One of the things I do remember with clarity is that Brother Larry kept trying to get in touch with me. He would phone and mail me notes and letters. I, however, pulled away.

Brother Larry didn't pressure me, though he must have sensed that something was off-kilter with me. He was always pleasant and polite and still trying to guide and mentor me spiritually. "How are you doing?" I always said I was fine. "How is work treating you?" I always said radio was keeping me busy, which was one way to put what was happening. "What are you up to outside of work?" I always kept my answers vague, uncontroversial, and inaccurate. "Do you want to get together to talk about life?" At this point, I never did. "Would you let me know if you need anything?" I always promised I would.

For some reason, after over four decades of knowing each other, Brother Larry's many patient efforts to reconnect with me during this part of my life remain in my memory and continue to inspire me. They are there as a trail of breadcrumbs waiting to guide me out of any dark forest I might happen to wander into. I have followed those breadcrumbs. However not following that trail back to Brother Larry several decades earlier is a bit of an embarrassment, one that I can only acknowledge with regret.

The night before Thanksgiving was always an opportunity to have some sort of a party. As I hit my late teens and early twenties, though, my definition of party had expanded to include a host of more exciting, more dangerous, and more shadowy distractions than any of the ones I enjoyed as a kid.

It's the night before Thanksgiving 1980, and I am prepping myself for a night of massive partying. I'm 22 years old, and I'm a disc jockey on my hometown radio station. I have access to just about any shadowy distractions I can possibly imagine. I imagine many different types of distractions because something deep inside my heart is confused, fearful, uncertain, and messed up. Perhaps it's anger at my abusive father for leaving the family. I felt it was up to me to take up the slack as the "man of the house" years before I should have been expected to. Maybe it's my mother's frequent drop-down bouts with alcohol. But, on this night before Thanksgiving 1980, none of that stuff seems to matter because I don't want those problems occupying my mind. The only thing I'm focusing on tonight is being out with my friends in Waterbury, Connecticut, and partying to the max.

We're bar-hopping all over town, going from one bar to the next. We are drinking up a storm, getting loaded. As we're driving from one hot spot to another, we're smoking pot, one joint after another. Truth be told, we are also snorting cocaine, a lot of it. Between the booze, the dope, and the coke, I'm getting blitzed and I'm driving! As the street signs rush by, some part of me knows that I am living dangerously. At some level, I am aware that I am incredibly stupid and irresponsible with my own life and other people's lives in the car. But another part of me doesn't care. After all, it's the night before Thanksgiving, one of the biggest party nights of the year. Time to let loose, right?

Now, it's very late in the night. I'm totally and completely blasted, driving when I know I shouldn't be, and I pull up in front of what has got to be, given the hour, the last bar of the night. The bartender's sour-faced expression confirms that we have just barely made it for the last call. We do a quick round of tequila, one shot apiece, and then the house lights go on, and we're rushed out of the place. We pile back into my car and decide we're going to go over to Stan's house (not his real name because I want to protect one of the participants in this partying fiasco). Stan's in the back seat, though I could have sworn that I started a conversation with him while he was sitting in the front. Apparently, there's been some shifting around of positions, guys and girls, girls and guys, whatever. Anyway, we're headed to Stan's place. That's where the evening drive is going to end, but the party is going to continue.

Somehow, we all get to Stan's place in one piece. We pile out of my car, and there I am on Stan's well-worn couch, smoking more dope and snorting more cocaine. After taking my deepest, longest snort from the mirror that's passed around, I drop the mirror.

Something weird has started happening inside my chest.

Stan notices the cocaine spilled all over the floor, and says, "What the hell, Stef??"

But spilled lines of cocaine are not a problem for me at this moment. Suddenly, my heart is beating fast...very, very fast. Too fast. I think to myself, *Wow. I'm really wasted.*

I stand up, ignoring the white powder on the carpet, and I say to Stan and everyone else, "I need to go outside for some fresh air." I stumble out onto Stan's porch.

I take a deep breath of the late autumn night air, thinking that's what I need to calm myself down. But even after that breath, my heart continues beating madly. The more I focus on it, the faster it beats. I think, *this heartbeat thing is getting out of control.* Now I'm sweating, and I'm getting concerned that something really is wrong with me.

Oh, my God. I'm having a heart attack.

I shout, "Stan, you have to drive me home. Now!"

Why I thought it made more sense for me to go home rather than to go to a hospital, I cannot tell you. Maybe I thought going to a hospital would let people know I wasn't the nice, polite, Catholic school-educated altar boy that I was projecting myself to be. Maybe there was some part of my brain that didn't want my mother to learn that I had died at Stan's house, surrounded by cocaine and marijuana. Who knows? I guess the human mind doesn't work very well when it's in the middle of a medical emergency and bombed with multiple controlled substances.

Stan and my other friends put me in the car. They bring me to my mother's house. I stumble upstairs, praying that no one will stop me on the way to my room. It's the night before Thanksgiving, and my heart is still racing as I enter my room. I realize that even though I am walking unsteadily and I still feel lousy, I'm home now, and that's some comfort because it is where I belong.

I stare into my bedroom mirror. I don't particularly like the look of the guy who stares back. He seems scared, distracted, unhappy, and ill. I shut my eyes because I don't want to look at his face. I close my eyes and pray in silence. *Dear God, don't let me die tonight.*

I mean it. If prayer helps, I'm going to pray. I repeat the prayer, out loud this time, but not too loud. I whisper it, so I don't wake anyone up. *Dear God, don't let me die tonight.*

I figure sleep may help. So, I get myself into bed, still fully clothed. The bed is spinning; the room is spinning; everything is spinning. Everything feels like it's out of control. My heart is still racing, and I begin to zone out. As I move into the land of crazy, paranoid, neurotic dreams, a thought crosses my mind. *If I were dying now, would I know it?*

Hours later, I wake up, and it's Thanksgiving morning. I can see the sun beaming through the window. I can smell the food that my mother is preparing downstairs. My first thought is, *I survived. I made it. I didn't have a heart attack, and I didn't have to go to the hospital. I didn't die. My mother didn't find me dead in my bed on Thanksgiving morning. Thank you, God! Thank you!*

I mean every word. I'm very grateful to God not to have died in my bed. I drag myself out of bed, hungover, feeling like I had been hit by a truck.

I go to the dresser drawer where I keep a baggie of pot, a bag of speed pills, and a vial of cocaine. I stumble into the bathroom, dump everything in the toilet and flush it all away. I make a promise to God and myself. Never again.

I shower and try to make myself look presentable for Thanksgiving. When I finally make it downstairs, my mother gives me half a smile, and a look that says, *Well, you had a big night last night, didn't you?* And I thought, *You don't know the half of it, Mama, and I hope you never do.*

Looking back, though, I'm wondering if maybe she did have some idea that I had just made a major decision. I wasn't very good at hiding things from her.

CHAPTER
NINETEEN

Thanksgiving 1980 was a turning point for me. It changed my whole way of living. I stopped smoking weed, stopped doing coke, and stopped taking speed. The only exception is an occasional social drink, which fortunately has never turned into a problem for me.

Most of the people who know me now think of me as the kind of person who wouldn't abuse drugs, and I am proud to be that kind of person today. But it's important for me now to own up to the reality that the person I was in my late teens and early twenties was the kind of person who abused drugs. It was a terrible choice, but it was how I coped with my problems.

Looking back, I'm not sure how I made it through that period, especially given what I know now about my heart condition. I guess I was very lucky, or very protected, or both. I have considered it something of a miracle that God answered my prayer that night.

A lot of things happened to me after Thanksgiving of 1980. Probably the most important was that I started taking Brother Larry up on his advice that we get together in person regularly. He would invite me to the Holy Cross Brothers' residence in Waterbury to talk about things and eat a meal together. He'd also invite me to be the guest speaker at the media class he continued to teach at Holy Cross High School.

Sometimes Brother Larry would come over to my mother's house for dinner and conversation. I started talking more openly with him about what was going on in my life. Just as important, I decided what wasn't going to be in my life anymore.

The regular talks with Brother Larry became a part of who I *was*. He asked me questions that I needed to hear. He wanted to know who I was as a person, what my spiritual life was like, and how my relationship with God was coming along? I didn't always have the best answers, but hearing Brother Larry pose the questions usually gave me a better sense of who I was supposed to be and what direction I should be heading. More times than I can count, I decided that he knew me as I knew myself, and maybe a little bit better.

The dark fog that was surrounding, suffocating, and defining me, lifted. I felt a whole lot better about my life. I think the talks with Brother Larry had a lot to do with it. With his help and guidance, I was eventually able to begin taking responsibility for the things that I could change in my own life and coming to terms with the things I couldn't change.

I eventually concluded that I couldn't change my mother's drinking problem. As that problem had gotten more entrenched over the years, I asked my mother for decades to stop drinking. I asked her to get help, to see someone, or to go to an AA meeting. Her reply had been, "Stefan, my drinking is not a problem. I can stop whenever I want because I'm the boss!"

For a long time, I had been resenting that answer, and disliking the inescapable reality that she was choosing *not* to stop drinking, regardless of the suffering that entailed for other people and for me. The talks with Brother Larry helped me come to terms with the fact that this was out of my hands. My best course was to find a way to make peace with my mother as she was, not as I wanted her to be.

My best path forward was to understand, to the degree that I could, what her life had been like, and to try to find a way to forgive her for the person she became when she was drinking. To accept sobriety had to be her choice, just as it had been mine. I don't think I could have ever gotten to the place in my life where that was possible without my talks with Brother Larry.

Once I did, decades later, another miracle occurred, one that I've already shared with you. It was the moment when my mother announced that she had stopped drinking as we were celebrating one of my birthdays. It was a powerful moment of connection, closeness, and acceptance with her—a moment I will always be grateful for and will never forget. What I didn't tell you earlier, what I didn't realize at the time, was that watching *Being There* and *Heaven Can Wait* with her on my birthday somehow led me into one of the darkest passages of my life.

Fourteen months later, my mother was diagnosed with lymphoma. She was terminally ill, and nothing could be done.

CHAPTER
TWENTY

Now into her late eighties, my mother Maria fell ill with lymphoma, a virulent form of cancer that begins in the immune system's infection-fighting cells and pretty much destroys everything in its path. It was a severe situation, and it scared me to the depth of my being. I cornered one of the head nurses at the nursing home where my mother was being taken care of and asked, "Give it to me straight. What's the diagnosis? What are we looking at?"

The nurse whispered, "I really shouldn't be telling you this, but since you've asked me so directly, I'm going to tell you. The doctor doesn't think your mother is going to make it through the weekend."

I asked this in such a way that my mother wouldn't be able to hear the conversation. Later that day, she asked me, "What does the doctor say?"

I wasn't going to lie to my mother. I took a deep breath, looked her in the eye, and said, "The doctor says he doesn't think you'll last the weekend."

The last thing in the world I expected my mother to do when she received that news was to smile, especially being in the greatly-weakened state that she was in. But, somehow, my mother did manage to smile, albeit very weakly, and said, "Tell the doctor he's wrong."

And you know what? She proved him wrong. My mother lived for seven more months. During those seven months, I visited her as often as I could, usually going up to Connecticut every Thursday and coming back to my home in New York on Sunday night. I could tell she was happy to have proved the doctors wrong. She had a certain look in her eye whenever she interacted with a nurse or a doctor during this period, a look that said, *God is running this show—not you.*

But in the late spring of 2013, it became clear to everyone, even to my mother, that although the doctors weren't running the show, the Man Upstairs definitely was, and He was giving every indication that the curtain was about to come down. Recognizing this, my mother sat me down and gave me a directive about my sister Jane.

"Stefan," she said, "you have all the information about my finances and access to all my accounts."

I nodded. It was true. I did.

"I don't know how much longer I'm going to make it. I want you to take whatever I have, cash everything in, and use the money to buy a home for Jane. I want you to do this as soon as you can so that I know she's settled in before I die. I want it to be a home for disabled women, and I want you to call it *Jane's Home*."

I told her I would get to work on that and do my best to make sure it all happened before she passed. At this stage, I had no idea what I was looking for or where the home was going to be.

To make sense of this next part of the story, you need to know that five years earlier, my mother and I had gone to a celebration in honor of Brother Larry. It was the 50th anniversary of his religious profession of vows as a Brother of Holy Cross. By now you now that he was one of my dearest and closest friends. My mother loved and admired him, too. During that festive celebration for Brother Larry, we happened to meet, and sit at the same table with a very charming Catholic priest by the name of Father Maurice Maroney. My mother and I chatted with Father Maroney and enjoyed his company immensely. We all had a lovely time together. I remember thinking, *There's something really special about that guy.*

Fast forward five years later. I've asked a real estate agent for help in finding a property that's suitable for *Jane's Home*. The real estate agent and I drove all around Waterbury, Connecticut, looking at prospective properties. There were 10 properties on her list that she wanted me to look at. So far, we've looked at seven of these houses, and none of them seemed appropriate to me. We pulled up to the eighth property, and something inside me whispered, *This is it.*

I got out of the car, looked around a bit, and the little voice was right. The place was perfect. It was as though it had been designed for Jane—which, in a way, it had. The last occupant, I learned, had been a developmentally disabled woman. Her brother had taken care of her and was now serving as the executor of the estate.

I said, "Make an offer."

The real estate agent said, "Are you sure? We have two more properties to see."

I said, "Nope, this is it. I know this is the place my mother would want me to buy. Make an offer."

The next day, the real estate agent called me with the details. Our offer has been accepted. The executor of the estate, Father Maurice Moroney, is looking forward to speaking with me.

I stared at the phone for a moment and said, "Would you say that name again?"

It turned out this was the very same Father Maurice Maroney that my mother and I just happened to meet five years earlier at Brother Larry's celebration!

CHAPTER
TWENTY-ONE

Revisiting my mother's life story in more detail than I ever did while she was alive has brought home a powerful truth for me. Sometimes we get what we want when we pray to God for help, and sometimes we don't.

This leads to some questions. Is the fact that prayer doesn't always seem to work, at least not from our limited human perspective, a justification for those who argue that it's random chance that governs our universe and not an all-seeing God who listens to us when we call out in need? Or, is this a sign of some more profound reality, some guiding principle that withholds and dispenses blessings in accordance with a plan that humans can't be expected to understand?

I realize these are big questions. I pose them not because I believe I can offer or prove any definitive answer, but because the point we've reached in my mother's story demands that they be asked. My own experience is that sometimes just *asking* a big question is essential, whether one has the answer or not. These questions matter more to me now as I confront my mother's mortality, and my own, with this book. They are worth taking the time to examine carefully.

My mother's journey did not always lead her to the destinations she prayed to reach. She was like all of us in that way. God didn't give her everything that she asked for. Often, He gave her the exact opposite. Yet, she didn't stop praying and didn't stop urging me to pray. Was she foolish to live like that? I don't think so.

I'm not a theologian or a moral philosopher. I probably couldn't hold my own in a debate with an aggressive, well-briefed atheist. I do believe, however, in my heart, that I have a Creator. For me, communicating with that Creator on a daily basis is a prerequisite of a happy, fulfilled life. I believe whenever something significant happens in my life, or whenever there is something I need help with, my first step is to talk to my Creator about that issue.

My mother believed those things, too, and even though neither of us could possibly prove what we thought to be true about God the Creator to the satisfaction of someone who believed the opposite, what I believe about God is true *for me*. Whether God answered my mother's prayers or mine in the manner we might have chosen is not the point. We come from God, and we return to God, and in the intervening time we pray to God, and one of the things we pray is *Thy will be done.*

I don't know why my mother had such a difficult life, why the difficulties she encountered did not decrease when she reached America. Why the many hardships she endured only strengthened her resolve and her reliance on God. Why the experience of facing a major medical emergency that put me face-to-face with the imminence and the inevitability of my own death brought me closer to my mother's faith commitment. And why the prospect of losing her made me more certain than ever that following her example when it came to prayer was the right thing to do—regardless of the outcome I encountered.

Here's what I do know. Prayer matters. It does have an impact. It shapes who you are, what you are capable of, and what you can bounce back from. I'm not the only one who knows that. I won't bore you with the details of all the research, but I will suggest that when you have time, search these phrases: *prayer and survival rates* and *prayer and longevity* into Google and see what comes back. One particularly striking study I found showed that total strangers praying for cardiac patients at San Francisco General Hospital had a significant positive effect on their recovery rates when compared with a control group of cardiac patients who had nobody praying for them.

I believe something positive happens when people appeal to their Creator. This doesn't mean the Creator always gives us what we want when we want it, but it does mean we can benefit from the communication. I believe we are well-advised to communicate with our Creator often. I believe there is a plan for each of us, and that prayer helps us align ourselves with it. We don't always know what the plan is, but God the Creator does.

I also believe prayer works. Prayer may not consistently deliver what *we* think we should receive on the timeline *we* prefer, but that's because God is not a short-order cook. I believe that we become better people when we pray, that we move closer to acceptance of God's plan for us, and that we move closer to being the kind of people we were meant to be.

Those are my takeaways. I'm confident they were my mother's as well.

I prayed as I had never prayed before for the strength to accept my mother's passing. I didn't want to lose her.

CHAPTER
TWENTY-TWO

By the end of September 2013, my mother had been in the nursing home for over six months. At that point, her health started to deteriorate. On one of my weekend visits to the nursing home, she looked me in the eye and said, "Stefan, I want to go home. I don't want to be here anymore."

I knew what lay underneath those words. My mother knew that she was dying, and she didn't want to die in the nursing home. She wanted to be in her own home when she passed.

On October 7, we signed my mother out of the nursing home. She went back to her own home to get the 24-hour-care she needed. We had a rotating shift of hospice nurses on hand to help take care of her, led by a wonderful home health aide named Violet. I got ready for the worst.

It was a grim and difficult month. I spent as much time with my mother as I could. Watching her decline made my body weak. I made frequent trips from Long Island to Connecticut and had a lot of trouble sleeping that month.

On Thursday, October 24, at about a quarter to seven in the morning, I sat at the kitchen table at my house, having breakfast with my wife, and I had the oddest feeling. Something strange was happening in my chest. It wasn't pain or a problem with the rhythm of my heart. It was just a feeling of something shifting.

The phone rang. It was Violet. She said, "Stefan, I'm here with your mother in her bedroom. She asked me to call you and your sister Barbara. She wants the two of you to come up here as soon as possible. She wants to see both of you right away."

I took a deep breath. The shifting thing in my heart, whatever it was, shifted again.

"Violet," I said, "could you please put my mother on the line?" This question came to me instantly. I think I must have wanted to be sure I heard my mother's voice and she heard mine if she passed away before I got there.

"Well, you might have a problem with that. Your mother's speech isn't very clear. But I'll put her on."

There was the sound of the phone being passed over, and then I heard my mother breathing. Her breaths were slow and labored.

I said in Polish, "Mama, this is Stefan. Violet says you want me to come up and see you now? Is that what you want me to do?"

The reply came back very faintly, in a rasping mumble, and very slurred. In Polish, she said: "Yes, I want you and Barbara to come here today."

In English this time, I said "Okay, Mama," and I hung up the phone. I called the office and let them know that I wouldn't be in for a couple of days. I called Barbara, and she said she'd drive up to Waterbury from her home in York, Pennsylvania as soon as she possibly could. I packed my bag, got in the car, and began the drive.

On the way, I listened to the radio because I didn't want to think about what I was driving towards. As fate would have it, the very first song that played was *My Maria* by B.W. Stevenson, which was a hit back in the fall of 1973.

My Maria...I've been longin' to see her...My Maria, I love you.

I burst out in tears.

At around 11:20 that morning, I pulled into the driveway of my mother's house, dashed inside, and immediately went into the room where she lay in bed.

In that faint voice, my mother kept saying that she was exhausted and sleepy, but she was glad that I was there. She kept repeating that as I sat next to her, holding her hand, and caressing her hair.

Barbara arrived just a little bit after me. The three of us, Barbara, Violet, and me, sat with my mother as she drifted in and out of what appeared to be sleeping.

During the afternoon, the visiting nurse showed up. She examined my mother and told us that she was in the process of actively dying. She also said that what we thought was my mother falling asleep and waking up was her drifting in and out of a coma.

The visiting nurse left.

We kept the vigil all night.

The morning of Friday, October 25 rolled around, and my mother didn't regain consciousness. While she appeared to be in a deep sleep, we knew that my mother was in a coma, based on what the nurse told us. Her breathing became more and more shallow.

Around 11 am, the visiting nurse came to the house again. She examined my mother, took her vital signs, and checked various points on her body. Even though she was under several blankets, her feet were cold, and the tips of her toes were starting to turn blue. The visiting nurse informed us this is one of the signs of imminent death.

At this point, Barbara was standing on one side holding one hand, and I was standing on the other side of the bed, holding my mother's other hand. As the minutes went by, my mother's breathing became more and more and more labored, and there were more significant and deeper pauses between her breaths.

At 11:47 a.m., when my mother took her last breath, I experienced something I never experienced before in my life and have not experienced since.

I felt an unmistakable jolt; it was like electricity but stronger. It went through my body. It started in my chest and shot right up through the top of my head. I gasped.

Once the sensation of being jolted had passed, I started weeping. Then I shouted out three words that I know must have come from somewhere, but I couldn't tell you where.

I shouted, "She made it!"

With tears of both joy and grief in my eyes, I felt as if I had walked my mother to the gates of Heaven while holding her hand. I sensed that she made it past the gate, and I could feel her spirit pass through me.

That is what I experienced. I hope you believe it because it's what happened. But that jolt passing through my body wasn't the only, or the biggest, miracle of my life.

CHAPTER
TWENTY-THREE

After my consultation with Doctor Leonard Girardi at his office in New York City, when I received the horrifying diagnosis that there was, and always had been, a shadow on my heart, I had the overwhelming urge to call my mother and talk to her about what had just happened to me. But of course, I couldn't. Maria had passed on a little over two years earlier. Somehow, for just an instant, I had allowed myself to forget that.

I think that's the way it is for a lot of us when we lose someone very close to us. Something important happens, and our first and deepest desire is merely to reach out to that person and share the experience, even though a part of your brain knows full well that you can't. I'm told that someone who has lost an arm or a leg feels pain, for a long time, in the place where the limb used to be. That's what it was like for me after I lost my mother. Whenever something significant happened to me, and I couldn't talk to her about it, I felt her loss all over again, and more keenly than ever.

Since I couldn't call my mother, I decided to do the next best thing. I decided to call Brother Larry. Part of the reason I did that connected to something that Doctor Girardi had suggested. As you may recall, he told me that I was facing serious, highly-invasive heart surgery and that the operation's outcome was by no means 100 percent certain. Since he considered himself to be operating in God's territory, he told me that he thought it might benefit me to speak to a spiritual counselor. Those were terrifying words to hear, and at first I pushed back against them. They seemed to confirm that I was in deep trouble. But later, when I was out of the doctor's office and being driven back home by my wife, having heard those words echoing in my head over and over again, and having realized that my mother was no longer around to give me the kind of guidance I wanted, I decided that I would follow the doctor's advice. I would call Brother Larry after my wife and I first told our children exactly what I was up against.

Brother Larry listened intently, and I struggled to get the words out. I had a genetic heart disease. The doctor is recommending open-heart surgery and that I should have it within the next week or two, at the latest. I needed a valve replacement and an aortic aneurysm repair. It would be a challenging recovery, and I needed a minimum of three months of recuperation.

On the other end of the phone line, I heard silence, and thought silently to myself, *Is Brother Larry even listening to me?*

Then, in a very calm voice, Brother Larry slowly asked, "So, how can I help you, Stefan?"

My brain went into a wild frenzy. I could barely concentrate on what I was saying and struggled to speak without bursting into tears, as a feeling of intense panic quickly grew inside.

I thought to myself, *How can you help me? My breast-bone is about to get sawed open. I'm going to get connected to a heart/lung machine that will keep me alive while they do one of the most serious operations anyone can undergo! You're my spiritual counselor, and you're asking me how you can help me?!?*

In his own unique, friendly, kind, but lovingly-firm way, Brother Larry challenged me to verbally express my faith. There was a part of me that knew that. Still, it was the last thing I wanted or expected. *Didn't Brother Larry know that I was a very sick man? Didn't he know I needed sympathy?* Even as these thoughts raced through my brain, there was a tone to Brother Larry's voice that seemed to say, *It's just me, Stefan. I've known you since you were a teenager in high school. You have nothing to hide.* And of course, I didn't. Brother Larry already knew all of my secrets. But I still found it difficult to say what we both knew I had called him for.

"I want you to help me pray for a miracle. I want you to pray that God will heal me so that I don't have to go through this surgery."

Another long pause from Brother Larry.

He then said, "Stefan, have you considered the possibility that the surgery *is* the miracle? That maybe you have to go through this difficult experience to *get* to the healing? I mean, maybe God will heal you the way you want. But Stefan, I'm thinking this surgery could be the miracle you're praying for, and you need to view it as that. Did you ever stop to consider that Jesus Christ had to be nailed to the cross to provide us with the miracle of His resurrection? Maybe this surgery is *your* resurrection. God gave you this, however it turns out, and God doesn't make mistakes. I think your mother would have agreed with that. Don't you?"

I listened to Brother Larry in disbelief. It was as if my mother were using his voice to tell me exactly what I needed to hear at this moment. Through Brother Larry, she'd found a way to get the message to me.

God's answer is always the best answer.

I began to cry, as Brother Larry prayed the *Our Father... Thy will be done.*

My mother was a simple woman. She was a farm girl who never graduated from high school because she was kidnapped and shipped off to Germany, where she was a slave laborer during the war. After the war, she met my father, got pregnant, got married, and found herself with a lot of domestic hardship to deal with. She never completed what we would consider a basic education. She saw things in black and white. She looked after her family. She inspired me to look for new and better ways to look after mine. If my mother had been on the phone with Brother Larry and me, and if I had asked her to explain the seemingly inexplicable trials of life that she had been forced to endure or explain the test I faced at that point in my life, I know she would have agreed with Brother Larry. I even know what words she would have used.

She would have said, "Stefan, God is your friend. He has always been there to help me. And He will be there to help you through this."

As I listened to Brother Larry pray the *Our Father*, I began to feel a sense of calmness and courage. I wanted God's blessing, no matter what my outcome was going to be.

CHAPTER
TWENTY-FOUR

One day, in the winter of 1965, a blizzard hit Waterbury. I was seven years old, and very excited about there being no school that day because of all the snow. My next-door-neighbor buddy Chris and I were out playing with our siblings and a bunch of our friends. We were sled riding down the street where we lived on Buckingham Street—it was a steep hill.

I suggested to Chris that we do a two-man sled ride down Buckingham. He wasn't sure that we should, but I was up for the challenge. I told Chris we'd be fine, got onto my sled, and invited him to get on. He did. One of the bigger kids gave us a push, and suddenly Chris and I were headed hurtling down the street, accelerating as we went.

All the boys at the top of the hill were shouting in excitement as we picked up speed. Chris said, "Oh, boy!"

The houses started moving past us in steadily blurrier forms. I soon realized, as I'm sure Chris must have, as we headed down Buckingham Street, that we were traveling as fast as we could on that rickety wooden sled of mine...*and faster* than we had ever gone before.

As we approached the base of the hill, which was where Buckingham Street intersected with Frederick Street, I heard Chris shout and scream, "Look!" I could see his gloved finger pointing toward our right.

I looked to the spot where Chris was pointing, and I saw what he saw. A car was headed down Frederick Street, toward roughly the same point as our sled.

"Jump!" Chris shouted.

And he didn't wait for a reply. He jumped off and tumbled into the soft snow on the slope to our right. But I thought I had a better idea. Being the seemingly invulnerable and brilliant 7-year-old that I thought I was, I decided that my sled was going so fast that I could beat the car across Frederick Street. Anyway, I didn't want to jump. That might hurt. And I couldn't stop anyway. So, I stayed on the sled.

The guy who was driving the car saw me on the sled and slammed on his brakes, but instead of slowing down or stopping, slamming the brakes actually caused his car to speed up as it skid on the snow and ice.

I saw the car coming, and I screamed, "Oh, God!" It's not much of a prayer, but I meant it. I wanted God to save me.

The car hit me, and there were all kinds of scraping and banging. My eyes closed and then opened, and I could see that I ended up getting wedged between the two front tires. We kept moving forward until the guy hit a patch of the street where there was no snow, and he was able to come to a stop.

The other boys from the top of the hill rushed down. The guy who was driving the car got out and rushed to the front as I climbed out from underneath the vehicle. My sled was completely mangled, but I didn't have a scratch on my body. It was unbelievable!

We walked to my house, where my mother came rushing out, trying to figure out what all the commotion was about. She immediately looked me over, found nothing wrong with me, but took me to Dr. Rosenberg, our family doctor, to make sure I was okay. She explained what happened. He examined me, then said, "Mrs. Rybak, there's nothing wrong with your son. There's not one scratch on his body. It's a miracle!"

My mother gave me a look that said, *Remember this moment.* It's not that she was angry with me, which is what I was expecting. She just wanted me to know that miracles *do* happen in life, and I had just experienced one.

When we got home, my mother took the mangled remains of the sled and hid it in the basement, where my father wouldn't see it. We both knew he'd instantly lose his temper and make both of our lives miserable if he found out what happened. When I ask her, years later, why she never told my father what happened, she looked at me, smiled, and said nothing. She just changed the subject.

I don't remember getting any lecture from my mother at the time about how stupid I was to sled ride down that hill. I don't remember her getting mad at me at all. But I do remember that look in the doctor's office. *It wasn't so much that she was urging me to pray for more miracles, it was more that she wanted me to understand that God had sent both of us on a journey, and that we had to be careful and responsible along the way because we never know exactly where that journey might take us. But wherever we ended up, we were protected by a kind, loving, and merciful God, who knows us better than we know ourselves.*

My mother said all that to me at the doctor's office without even saying a word. I believed it then, and I still do, especially after the miracle of my heart surgery. I wrote this book because I wanted to share that lesson with you. Perhaps, when the time is right, you'll feel like sharing it with someone you love.

ABOUT THE AUTHOR

Stefan Rybak is an energetic, enthusiastic, positively motivated, and highly experienced multimedia management professional with a 40-year track record of proven success and expertise in radio, television, and print and digital media.

Stefan's background and experience includes advertising, marketing, sales, sales management, management consulting, new media, and professional speaking.

Stefan has written over 500 published articles and won the *Billboard* Magazine "Program/Operations Director of the Year" award two consecutive years.

He lives in the greater New York City area with his family.